The Little Gothic Bakeshop

Over 50 Recipes with Sweetness and Shadows in Every Bite

Helena Garcia

castle

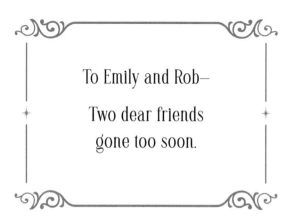

To Emily and Rob—

Two dear friends
gone too soon.

CONTENTS

Spooky Cookies and Candies · 17

Ghoulish Breads and Pastries · 45

To-Die-For Desserts · 79

Macabre Cakes and Bakes · 109

Bewitching Beverages · 139

Introduction

Welcome witches, vampires, ghouls, and goblins to my hauntingly delicious bakery! For those who don't know me, my name is Helena Garcia, a self-confessed kitchen witch who once appeared in a lovely little baking show in the United Kingdom called *The Great British Bake Off* (also known as *The Great British Baking Show* in the United States).

It's been five years since my appearance on the show, five magical years full of incredible experiences. I was immediately cast to make a cameo appearance in a show about a bunch of dysfunctional vampires living in Staten Island. Then came my first baking book, *The Wicked Baker*, followed by another two, and a children's storybook in between. What all these books have in common is my love for all things dark, spooky, witchy, and, above all, stylish and sophisticated, because one look does not deny the other.

My love for baking comes from a very early age. I got involved in the kitchen every time my grandmother—who cooked everything from scratch (she even pasteurized her own milk!)—would cook a meal. However, as I entered my teenage years, baking rather than cooking became my favorite pastime. Baking offered me the opportunity to create a world where the allure of the macabre met the magic of the culinary realm. Make no mistake—putting ingredients into a bowl and turning them into a baked good is indeed magic!

It has now been two years since I published my last book, *The Book of Gingerbread*, and I've had a little break from recipe development to fill my brain with new inspiration. But truth be told it is old inspiration and dreams of bakes of the past that come back to haunt me, from rich spiced cakes that evoke the warmth of a lit kitchen stove to classic French pastries adorned with sinister swirls.

Most bakers dream of two things: publishing a book and having their own little local bakery. In a way *The Little Gothic Bakeshop* covers both dreams for me. The recipes in this book are essentially what my first little gothic bakery would offer. From small whimsical treats like naughty chocolate black cats or pistachio-filled frogs, to spookified traditional breads like fougasse or brioche, my bakery would whip up delicious indulgences with a goth glam style for any time of the year. Think Kram-Puss cookies for Gothmastime, Scary Teddy celebration cakes for birthdays, or mini pavlovas of peril. And of course, no bakery would be complete without an offering of bewitching beverages, including extraordinary teas, mysterious potions, and alchemist cocktails.

In my mind, my dream bakery looks traditional at first, but when you dig deeper the unique and charming details start to emerge. Lit candelabras adorn the serving counter, trays of ghoulish baked goods displayed in the Victorian curved windows, cauldrons stacked up on the shelves, and vintage chandeliers with flickering bulbs to create a dark and delightful atmosphere—situated on a quiet cobbled street with medieval-era buildings and sunken Tudor houses with blackened wooden beams (I am practically describing The Shambles in York, UK, believed to have inspired Diagon Alley in the Harry Potter books).

This bakery is open to serve ghostly offerings all year round, from Halloween and Fangsgiving through Witchmas, St. Pa-trick-or-treat to Summerween. The flavors of the bakes of course reflect the changing seasons. Pumpkin, maple, cinnamon, pecan, and ginger are staples of autumn-winter baking, but in my bakery, we also celebrate lemon, strawberry, coffee, peanut butter, and pistachio, to name just a few. And although there are plenty of sweet offerings, we also have haunting savory breads and pastries like devil's fingers sausage rolls, bat-shaped fougasse, or potato bread horror clowns.

Perhaps this book will be the push I need to open my own gothic bakeshop someday. But for now, *The Little Gothic Bakeshop* invites you into my kitchen to learn all my tips and tricks for creating the most entertaining goth bake spread ever. Lean into your dark side and use these spell-like recipes to turn everyday bakes into your wildest gothic dreams.

Bone appétit! Something creepy this way comes!

Gothic Living
In the Kitchen and Beyond

As a self-confessed witch obsessed with pagan practices, the darker side of popular culture, and folklore with a little sprinkle of the macabre, I have always been attracted to the gothic aesthetic.

Gothic lifestyle can be traced back to the Visigoths of history, the prevalence of Gothic architecture across Europe, the adoration of the gothic literature genre, and the dress and obsession with death of the Victorian Age. The culture which we recognize today began in the early 1980s as part of the post-punk movement. Rooted in an appreciation for, let's just say, the melancholic side of life, being goth is characterized by dramatic fashion (black clothing, dark makeup, and Victorian-inspired styles), an introspective mindset, and a deep love for the unusual, supernatural, and mysterious. The goth subculture truly took hold through the music scene with bands like Bauhaus, Siouxsie and the Banshees, and The Cure, whose music expressed themes of alienation, melancholy, and romanticism.

The gothic aesthetic quickly spread beyond music into fashion, art, cinema, and all aspects of life, emphasizing individuality, self-expression, and an appreciation of beauty in darkness. It challenges conventional norms and celebrates the strange, the different, and the forgotten. For me, this is not just a passing trend or a phase—it's a fundamental part of who I am.

My approach and influence from the gothic movement is somewhat eclectic, especially when it comes to my personal style. Venturing beyond external looks, it's a way of life that shapes how I express myself creatively. In my baking, for example, I like to embrace the darker side of beauty; sometimes this leads to more complicated recipes, but not always. I like to present goods that are not only unique but deeply personal and full of meaning.

Take the Spiderweb Galette des Rois and Black Widow Profiteroles for example. These aren't simply Christmas bakes with a gothic twist—they tell a story. In the heartwarming Eastern European story of the Christmas spider, legend says that a widowed mother had no money to decorate the Christmas tree for her children, so a friendly spider came down from the attic to create elaborate cobwebs all over the evergreen.

On Christmas morning, the mother and her children woke up, opened the curtains and when the sunlight hit the spiderwebs, they turned silver and gold and that's where, they say, the tradition of decorating the tree with tinsel at Christmas comes from. Baking, like gothic culture, is a form of self-expression. Art that you can eat!

When it comes to my personal fashion or interior decorating style, I put my own spin on the gothic look by blending vintage or classic pieces with modern twists. And . . . get ready to be shocked . . . I'm not afraid of or opposed to color either! At home I love to introduce elements of antique furniture and accessories with practical features. For example, my kitchen island is made from a Victorian set of apothecary drawers. Storage units that once held medicinal herbs and powders are now filled with cookie cutters, an array of flavoring extracts, and other baking ingredients.

People who embrace the goth movement embrace complexity. We know we do not need to "fit in" to be valued or successful. The world is changing, and individuality is encouraged and celebrated. So don't be afraid to take a walk through the darker side of life!

The Gothic Pantry

The home baker always wants to have the following staples in their pantry:

All-purpose flour

Assorted chocolate bars and morsels (dark, milk, white)

Baking powder

Baking soda

Bread flour

Brown sugar (light and dark)

Citrus for zesting (lemon, orange, lime)

Cocoa powder

Condensed milk

Corn starch

Cream cheese

Flavoring extracts (vanilla, almond, anise, etc.)

Freshly ground black pepper

Gelatin (animal or plant-based)

Granulated white sugar

Heavy whipping cream

Nonstick cooking spray

Oils (olive, coconut, vegetable, sesame, etc.)

Plant-based milks (almond, oat, cashew, etc.)

Powdered sugar (also known as confectioners' or icing sugar)

Rice flour

Sea salt

Semi-sweet chocolate chips

Standard dairy, like eggs and butter (both salted and unsalted)

Vanilla bean pods

Variety of nuts (almonds, pecans, walnuts, etc.)

Variety of seeds and nuts (poppy, sesame, sunflower, etc.)

Whole milk

Yeast (instant dry or fast-acting)

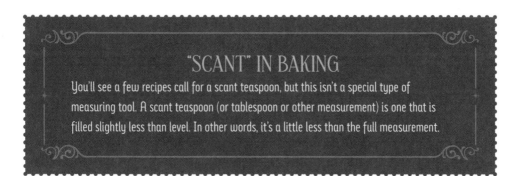

"SCANT" IN BAKING

You'll see a few recipes call for a scant teaspoon, but this isn't a special type of measuring tool. A scant teaspoon (or tablespoon or other measurement) is one that is filled slightly less than level. In other words, it's a little less than the full measurement.

If you're getting more creative and adventurous with your bakes, you'll need the following to create bakeshop-level decorations, especially when it comes to all the gory and spooky designs in this book. There are also certain flavor profiles that align well with gothic baking.

Autumnal spices (cinnamon, clove, ginger, nutmeg, allspice, pumpkin, apple)

Candy melts

Edible ink pens in various colors

Espresso powder or brewed espresso/coffee

Food coloring in various shades

Fondant

Herbs and edible flowers (lavender, rose, rosemary, thyme, etc.)

Isomalt

Luster dust in a variety of colors, especially red and black

Maple syrup

Marzipan

Modelling chocolate

Molasses

Nut butters (hazelnut, pistachio, etc.)

Piping gel

Premade spooky-shaped decorations, like sprinkles or candy in the shape of bones, bats, witch hats, cats, pumpkins, etc.

Royal icing

Superfine sugar (also known as caster)

MAKE YOUR OWN TEMPLATES

If you can't find a cookie cutter in the shape or size you need, you can make your own traceable shapes. Find a black outline drawing of your desired shape online, print to size (this might take some troubleshooting with scaling to a percentage), paste or tape to thin-but-sturdy cardboard, and cut out. Tape around the perimeter of your template for easy gliding with your knife!

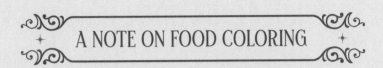

A NOTE ON FOOD COLORING

The amount of food coloring used will depend on the shade you desire to achieve. Some of the recipes here will give direction on the shade to aim for, but mostly it will be up to you. Add less for lighter shades and more for deeper shades. You always want to start out with a few drops and then add little by little. You can always add more, but you can't take away if you overdo it! And remember—be generous when adding color to doughs that go into the oven, as color always fades during baking.

Gel food coloring versus liquid food coloring . . . does it make a difference? Absolutely! Gel food coloring is highly concentrated, while liquid food coloring is more diluted. Because of this, gel food coloring will give you intense colors with small amounts, which is important for use in recipes like frosting or fondant to avoid major changes in texture. It's better to use liquid food coloring for batters and doughs where you are less concerned about adding extra liquid.

And what about water-based versus oil-based food coloring? Similar to whether to use gel or liquid, you'll want to use water-based or oil-based food coloring depending on what you're making. Water-based food coloring will dissolve in water so it's best to use in recipes that are meant to be light and airy such as frostings, icings, macaroons, meringues, or jellies. Oil-based food coloring dissolves best in fat or butter so save them for chocolate, candy melts, buttercreams, and ganaches.

Essential Tools and Equipment

You most likely have many of these items already in your kitchen, but a few on the list may surprise you. These specialty kitchen gadgets make quick work of some processes and give your bakes a professional, clean look.

Airbrush kit

Baking pans in a variety of sizes (most common being 9-inch, 23-cm round)

Baking sheets in a variety of sizes (most common being 9 by 13 inches, 23 by 34 cm)

Candy thermometer

Cookie cutters in various shapes (like moons, stars, circles, etc.)

Culinary blowtorch

Double boiler

Electric stand mixer with attachments (paddle, whisk, hook)

Food processor

Ice-cream maker

Kitchen twine

Measuring cups

Measuring spoons

Microwave-safe bowls

Mixing bowls in a variety of sizes

Paper cake pop or lollipop sticks

Parchment paper

Pastry bags (also known as piping bags) with a variety of tips in multiple sizes and shapes

Pastry brushes (silicone and bristles)

Pie weights (can also use dry beans or rice)

Plastic wrap

Polystyrene or Styrofoam cones and blocks

Ramekins

Rolling pin

Ruler or measuring tape

Saucepans in a variety of sizes

Scale

Scissors and sharpener

Skewers

Silicone baking mats

Silicone spatulas

Spooky-themed silicone molds (cauldrons, cats, pumpkins, etc.)

Toothpicks

Wooden dowels or rods

Wooden spoons

HOW TO MAKE
FOOD-GRADE SILICONE MOLDS

Silicone molds have made highly decorated cakes and bakes a hell of a lot easier to make. There was a time when most of these decorations were either piped in royal icing or wooden blocks were carved individually to make molds. These days you can type almost anything into Google and you're guaranteed to get a silicone mold in that shape, and they're incredibly affordable as well. However, if you ever feel you can't find what you need or wish to create your own, here is a quick and easy recipe.

You will need:
- Food-safe silicone rubber, such as PlatSil 73-60
- Plastic container
- Object you want to make a mold of

1. Clean the object you have chosen to mold with soap and water and dry completely.
2. Place the object in a plastic container slightly larger than the object.
3. Mix both parts of the food-safe silicone rubber according to manufacturer's instructions, then pour into the container, around the object you want to mold.
4. Let dry until firm.
5. Once fully dry, unfold carefully.

TIP Alternatively you can use Alumilite's Amazing Mold Putty, another two-part molding material. It's the consistency of plasticine so you knead it together, mold it around your object, and let it set for around an hour. This method is easier and quicker, but the detailing of the object isn't as sharp.

Spooky Cookies and Candies

Chocolate Spiderweb Sand-Witch Cookies

YIELD: 15 sandwich cookies ♀ PREP TIME: 45 minutes, plus 60 minutes chill time ♀ BAKE TIME: 8 to 10 minutes

COOKIE DOUGH

1 ¼ cups (160 g) all-purpose flour,
plus extra for dusting
½ cup (50 g) black cocoa powder
(see Note)
½ teaspoon baking soda
⅛ teaspoon baking powder
¼ teaspoon sea salt
1 cup (195 g) superfine sugar
½ cup plus 2 tablespoons (140 g)
vegan butter, at room temperature
1 teaspoon vanilla extract
4 to 5 tablespoons oat milk

VANILLA FILLING

⅓ cup (70 g) coconut oil,
softened if it has hardened
1 cup (100 g) powdered sugar, sifted
½ teaspoon vanilla extract

This witch's take on Oreo cookies is, as expected, a bit more eerie, but just as delicious as its inspiration. My homemade version sticks to the original cookie's vegan properties and ups the spooky factor with a fancy spiderweb decoration. To achieve the design simply score it with a sharp knife, or you can make the process go much quicker with a spiderweb cookie stamp.

1. To make the cookie dough: In a large bowl, combine the flour, cocoa powder, baking soda, baking powder, and salt and set aside.

2. In the bowl of an electric mixer fitted with the paddle attachment, beat the superfine sugar with the butter on medium-high speed until light and fluffy. Add the vanilla and mix until combined.

3. Add the dry ingredients and mix on low speed. Then gradually add the milk until you get a cookie dough consistency (you may not need all the liquid).

4. Turn the dough out onto a clean surface and bring together with your hands, flatten slightly, and wrap in plastic wrap. Refrigerate for 45 minutes.

5. Preheat the oven to 375°F (190°C) and line two baking sheets with parchment paper.

6. On a lightly floured surface, roll out the cookie dough to a 1/8- to 1/16-inch (2 to 3 mm) thickness.

7. If scoring the spiderweb design by hand, use a 1 3/4-inch (4 1/2 cm) diameter cookie cutter to cut out 30 cookies. Then score a spiderweb design on each with a sharp knife. If using a spiderweb stamp, stamp the dough leaving enough space between the stamps to cut a circle around the spiderweb designs with your cookie cutter.

8. Place the cookies on the prepared baking sheets and refrigerate for another 15 minutes. Bake for 8 to 10 minutes. Leave to cool on a wire rack.

9. To make the filling: In the bowl of an electric mixer fitted with the paddle attachment beat the coconut oil until light and fluffy. If it has hardened, warm up prior to beating in the microwave for a few seconds. Add the powdered sugar and vanilla. Continue mixing until well combined.

10. Once the cookies are fully cooled, spread a thin layer of the filling on the inside of one cookie and top with another. Continue with the remaining cookies and filling.

NOTE Black cocoa powder is more heavily Dutched (or alkalized) than regular cocoa powder. It has a lovely, smooth, non-bitter taste, but tastes much less chocolatey, which makes way for the cookie filling to be the star.

TIP If you don't have or don't like oat milk, you can use or any other plant-based milk in this recipe.

Kinder® Malo Kitties

YIELD: 16 kitties • PREP TIME: 35 minutes • CHILL TIME: Overnight, plus 30 minutes

DOUGH BALLS

1/3 cup plus 1 1/2 tablespoons (100 ml) whole milk
1/2 cup (80 g) pitted Medjool dates
6 tablespoons (50 g) milk powder
1/2 cup (120 ml) hazelnut butter
1 teaspoon vanilla extract
1 bar (9 ounces, or 250 g) dark or milk chocolate,
    such as Lindt

DECORATION

32 mini dark chocolate chips
16 heart-shaped sprinkles, pink or red
White edible ink pen

Kinder® Buenos are one of my favorite chocolate bars. I love American candy, but when it comes to chocolate, it must be European. *Bueno* means good in Spanish, and the opposite is *malo*. Styled to look like everyone's favorite Spooky Season feline, my Kinder® Malo Kitties are the evil twin chocolate versions of the Kinder® Buenos. These treats are in fact better for you as they have no sugar; they're sweetened with dates instead, so maybe not so *malo* after all!

1. To make the dough balls: In a small saucepan, add the milk and warm up over medium heat to just before boiling.

2. In a food processor, combine the milk, dates, milk powder, hazelnut butter, and vanilla and blend until combined. Pour into a medium-sized container with a lid and refrigerate for 8 hours or overnight.

3. Scoop out the mixture and roll into 1-inch (3 cm) balls. Place them on a baking sheet lined with parchment paper and freeze for 30 minutes.

4. Meanwhile, prepare the chocolate. In a microwave-safe bowl, melt the chocolate bar in the microwave at 30-second intervals, stirring in between. Pour approximately 1/4 cup (60 ml) of the chocolate into a pastry bag and pipe the shape of cat tails onto a silicone mat or parchment paper.

5. While the tails set, take the balls out of the freezer and dip them one by one into the remaining melted chocolate using a fork to help coat fully. Shake off the excess and put them back onto the tray.

6. To decorate: Once the chocolate is set on the balls, add the tails, two chocolate chips for ears, and one heart-shaped sprinkle for the nose, securing them all with a little of the melted chocolate you have left. Draw the whiskers on opposite sides of the nose with the white edible ink pen.

NOTE | There are many types of milk powder options (even vegan!), so choose which works best for you. The results of the recipe will be the same.

Mini Gingerbread Haunted Houses

xxxxxxxxxxxxxxxxxxxxxxxxxxxxxxxxxxxxxxxxxxxxxxxxxxxxxxxxxxxxxxxxxxxxxxxxx

YIELD: 12 houses ⚜ PREP TIME: 1 ½ hours, plus 30 minutes chill time ⚜ BAKE TIME: 12 to 14 minutes

GINGERBREAD DOUGH

2 cups (250 g) all-purpose flour,
    plus extra for dusting
1 teaspoon baking soda
2 teaspoons ground ginger
1 teaspoon ground cinnamon
1/4 teaspoon ground cloves
1/4 teaspoon sea salt
1/2 cup plus 1 tablespoon (125 g)
    unsalted butter, at room temperature
1 cup (220 g) packed brown sugar
1 medium egg
1/4 cup (60 ml) molasses

DECORATION

Royal icing
Black-colored frosting
Candy corn
Orange-colored frosting
Purple-colored frosting
Green-colored frosting
Spooky sprinkles like bones,
    bats, and more

I've seen these lovely little gingerbread houses that sit on the rim of a cup of hot cocoa for Christmas, so why not make a Halloween version? Cutting the house shape is made easy when you use the template (scan the QR code to download!), but when it comes to decorating, get creative! I've gone for both a classic holiday black-and-orange look and a more witchy-goth look here, but the possibilities are endless. This is your opportunity to design your own little gingerbread house of horrors!

1. To make the dough: In a large bowl, combine the flour, baking soda, ginger, cinnamon, cloves, and salt. Set aside.

2. To an electric mixer fitted with the paddle attachment, add the butter and sugar and beat on medium-high speed until well mixed (or alternatively mix by hand with a wooden spoon).

3. Add the egg and molasses to the butter mixture and mix well. Then add the flour mixture and continue mixing to just bring it together.

(continued on next page)

(continued from previous page)

4.   Tip the dough out onto a clean surface and knead slightly until smooth. Flatten, wrap in plastic wrap, and refrigerate for 30 minutes.

5.   Preheat the oven to 325°F (165°C) and line two baking sheets with parchment paper.

6.   On a lightly floured surface, roll out the dough to a ¼-inch (½-cm) thickness. Use the template to cut out the house pieces and place on the prepared baking sheets 2 inches apart.

7.   Bake for 12 to 14 minutes, or until golden brown. Leave to cool on a wire rack.

8.   To assemble: Stick the house walls and roof together using the royal icing and leave to set before decorating.

9.   To decorate: For a classic holiday house, pipe black-colored frosting on the roof to create tiles and attach a candy corn at the top. Then pipe a few windows using the orange-colored frosting and add a few spiderwebs using the royal icing.

10. For a second witchy-gothic cottage variation, pipe the purple-colored frosting to create roof tiles and windows, and pipe the green-colored frosting to create climbing ivy. Add spooky sprinkles where desired.

TIPS

If you don't have or don't like molasses, you can substitute with golden syrup, honey, maple syrup, or corn syrup.

Since we're using such small amounts, store-bought frosting is ok for the decorations. If finding precolored frosting proves difficult, you can dye plain vanilla frosting with food coloring in your choice of colors.

Scary Teddy Chocolate Chip Cookies

YIELD: 14 to 16 scary teddys   ♦   PREP TIME: 10 minutes   ♦   BAKE TIME: 8 to 9 minutes

1 ¹⁄₂ cups (190 g) all-purpose flour
¹⁄₂ teaspoon baking soda
¹⁄₄ teaspoon baking powder
¹⁄₂ teaspoon sea salt
¹⁄₂ cup (115 g) salted butter
¹⁄₂ cup (100 g) superfine sugar
¹⁄₂ cup (100 g) packed light brown sugar
1 teaspoon vanilla extract
1 large egg
1 cup (175 g) chocolate chips, divided
Red luster dust
Royal icing
Red food coloring

Everyone has a favorite chocolate chip cookie recipe! But taking an innocent teddy bear shape and removing the eyes and nose and giving it a large open mouth with pointy teeth makes this formerly cuddly friend and nostalgic treat downright terrifying. But not scary enough to stop me from making a cake version (page 135)!

1. Preheat the oven to 375°F (190°C) and line two baking sheets with silicone mats or parchment paper.

2. In a medium bowl, combine the flour, baking soda, baking powder, and salt. Set aside.

3. In the bowl of an electric mixer fitted with the paddle attachment, cream the butter and sugars together on medium speed until light and fluffy, 2 to 3 minutes.

4. Add the vanilla and egg and continue mixing until fully incorporated.

5. Add the dry ingredient mixture and mix on low speed, scraping down the sides and bottom of the bowl if necessary.

6. Add ¹⁄₂ cup (85 g) chocolate chips and mix until just incorporated. Do not overmix.

(continued on page 27)

(continued from page 25)

7. Roll a scoop of cookie dough into a 1 ½-inch (3.8 cm) ball for the teddy bear face and two smaller scoops for the ears. Press them slightly onto the parchment paper. Repeat with the rest of the dough, spacing them evenly on the baking sheets.

8. Add the rest of the chocolate chips randomly on the teddy bears avoiding the mouth area.

9. Put the trays in the freezer while you wait for the oven to preheat. This will ensure they keep their shape well.

10. Bake for 8 to 9 minutes, just until they start to brown at the edges.

11. Remove and let cool for 2 minutes before using a ball modelling tool (or your thumb) to create a big open mouth shape. This needs to be done while the cookies are still warm.

12. After shaping the mouths, let the cookies cool completely. Then brush the red luster dust on the inside of the mouth and pipe in sharp, scary teeth with the royal icing.

13. Once the icing sets, add drops of red food coloring to make it look like blood is streaming down the scary teddy's teeth.

NOTE | A chocolate chip cookie recipe is very personal. Luckily, this decorating idea is simple and very effective so feel free to use your family recipe and get the same, horrifying results.

Victorian Doll-Face Candy Apples

YIELD: 14 to 16 doll faces ♀ PREP TIME: 10 minutes ♀ REST TIME: 20 minutes

14 to 16 small apples
14 to 16 wooden sticks
2 cups (400 g) granulated sugar
¼ cup (60 ml) corn syrup
   or golden syrup
Red food coloring

Candy apples are so easy to make, and the addition of a doll face gives that extra creepy factor we all know dolls embody. The doll-face molds are a steal on eBay! Depending on the size of the molds you use, you may get less or more in terms of yield. Make sure to use small apples so they fit the mold size; in my supermarket they sell them as "kids' apples." But if they're in season, go to an orchard and pick your own! Somehow, apples always taste better if you've picked them yourself.

1. Remove the apple stems and insert sticks in their place. Set aside.

2. In a large saucepan, combine the sugar, syrup, and ¾ cup (174 ml) of water. Bring to a boil over medium-high heat then turn the heat slightly down so it doesn't boil over. Mix in the red food coloring.

3. Insert a candy thermometer and continue to boil until the mixture reaches the hard crack stage, 300° to 310°F (149° to 154°C).

4. After 15 to 20 minutes, remove pan from the heat and let it cool for 5 minutes, or until the bubbles have subsided.

5. Dip the apples one at a time into the mixture until they are fully coated. Turn each apple to its side and insert into the mold so the excess sugar mixture fills the shape. If there's not enough of the sugar mixture on the apple, add a little to the mold prior to placing the coated apple inside.

6. Let it cool for 15-20 minutes, then remove from the mold carefully and display on a tray.

TIP ┃ You can buy the sticks in bamboo or even heavy paper (like those used for cake pops), but I normally pick and clean sticks that have fallen off tree branches in my yard. To be food safe, remove the bark from the end that gets inserted into the apples.

Pumpkin Spice Truffles

YIELD: 35 truffles ☙ PREP TIME: 1 hour 15 minutes ☙ CHILL TIME: 2 hours

6 ounces (170 g) graham crackers
2 ounces (60 g) cream cheese,
    at room temperature
2 tablespoons powdered sugar
2 ½ ounces (70 g) pumpkin purée
½ teaspoon pumpkin-pie spice
½ teaspoon ground cinnamon
Superfine sugar for rolling
35 chocolate chips for stems

These little beauties can be used as cake decorations, for a Halloween-themed dessert platter, or just eaten on their own! If you are not fussed about them looking like pumpkins, you can skip the ridge detail and instead of rolling them in sugar, dip them in melted white chocolate that has been dyed orange with food coloring (see Note).

1. In a food processor, add the graham crackers and pulse until they resemble breadcrumbs. Add the cream cheese, sugar, pumpkin purée, pumpkin-pie spice, and cinnamon and pulse until well combined.

2. Refrigerate the mixture for 2 hours.

3. Use your hands to roll the mixture into balls about an inch in diameter. Fill a bowl with superfine sugar and roll the balls through, making sure each is completely covered. Place on a silicone mat or parchment paper. Using a toothpick, draw the familiar ridges of a pumpkin from top to bottom all around each ball.

4. Top each pumpkin with a chocolate chip for the stalk and enjoy!

NOTE | If choosing the chocolate-dipped option, you'll need about 4 ounces (115 g) white chocolate. The amount of orange food coloring depends on the shade of orange you are looking to achieve.

Vampire's Bloody Valentine Lollipops

YIELD: 12 to 14 bloody lollipops ❧ PREP TIME: 15 minutes ❧ SET TIME: 10 minutes

12 to 14 lollipop sticks
2 cups (400 g) granulated sugar
2/3 cup (160 ml) light corn syrup
1/4 cup (60 ml) water
2 teaspoons cherry extract
Red food coloring

If you've never made your own lollipops, I can assure you it's so incredibly easy and affordable that you'll start making them all the time. The red food coloring mixed into the sugar really does look like drops of blood, a very attractive quality for our vampy friends. For flavor I've used cherry, but you can use whatever perks up your fangs. These lollies make for the perfect Valentine's Day gift, or any time you want to show your undead love for another.

1. Prepare two baking sheets with silicone mats or parchment paper and arrange the lollipop sticks 3 inches apart.

2. In a medium saucepan, combine the sugar, corn syrup, and water and bring to a boil over medium heat. Stir with a spatula until all the sugar has dissolved.

3. Put a candy thermometer in the pan and bring the mixture to the hard crack stage, 300° to 310°F (149° to 154°C).

4. Immediately remove the sugar mixture from the heat and place into an ice bath to stop the cooking process. Be careful as the pan will steam up and be hot. Let the pan cool down until it stops steaming, about 5 minutes.

5. Add the cherry extract and mix.
6. Working quickly, pour the syrup mixture onto the trays forming 3-inch circles over the top end of each stick.
7. Working one lollipop at a time, squirt a few drops of the red food coloring in the center and swirl it around with a toothpick. Don't swirl it too much as you want the "blood" to look coagulated.
8. Let the lollipops harden completely then gently separate them from the trays.

NOTE | Since you will be making the lollipops freehand (not using a mold), you may get less or more in terms of yield.

TIP | To give these bloody good lollies as gifts, wrap them in cellophane bags tied up with red ribbon and a little fang charm.

Kanafeh Chocolate Frogs

YIELD: 16 frogs ❖ PREP TIME: 15 minutes ❖ CHILL TIME: 60 minutes

PISTACHIO BUTTER

7.5 ounces (200 g) pistachios,
   peeled and toasted
1 tablespoon vegetable oil

KANAFEH FILLING

2 tablespoons unsalted butter
3/4 cup (65 g) kanafeh pastry, chopped
   into 1/3-inch (1-cm) strands
1/4 cup (60 ml) tahini
2 tablespoons powdered sugar

CHOCOLATE COATING

3 bars (300 g) Lindt milk chocolate,
   chopped

DECORATION

Gold luster dust

You may have seen the viral Dubai chocolate bar filled with kataifi or kanafeh pastry and pistachio cream. Is it worth the hype? It is, especially when in frog form! Kanafeh is basically shredded filo pastry, which can be found in local Southeast Asian supermarkets and is also widely available online. I've tried this filling using semi-sweet, milk, and white chocolate, and my preference is the milk chocolate so that is what is included here. But feel free to change it up per your own preference!

1. To make the pistachio butter: In a food processor, combine the pistachios and oil and blend until it becomes the consistency of a spreadable nut butter. You will end up with 3/4 cup (180 ml) pistachio butter.

2. To make the filling: In a medium pan, melt the butter over medium heat. Toss in the pastry and cook until toasted, stirring constantly to avoid burning.

3. Pour the toasted pastry into a bowl and mix in the tahini and powdered sugar. Mix in the pistachio butter and set aside.

4. To prepare the coating: In a microwave safe bowl, add the chocolate pieces and melt in the microwave at 30 second intervals. Stir well in between with a spatula.

(continued on next page)

(continued from previous page)

5. Pour a thin layer of chocolate into the 2.75-inch (or 7-cm) frog molds making sure to spread it all the way to the top. Using a silicone brush helps to do this. Refrigerate until set, about 30 minutes.

6. Remove from the refrigerator and fill the frogs with the kanafeh-pistachio filling and top with another layer of chocolate. You may have to reheat your chocolate in the microwave if it has hardened too much to pour.

7. Refrigerate until set, around 30 minutes.

8. To decorate: Remove from the refrigerator and unmold. Brush them with gold luster dust using a pastry brush with bristles.

Kram-Puss Chocolate Cookies

YIELD: 48 cookies ⚲ PREP TIME: 15 minutes, plus 2 hours and 15 mintues chill time ⚲ BAKE TIME: 7 to 9 minutes

2 cups (250 g) all-purpose flour

½ cup (50 g) cocoa powder

1 teaspoon sea salt

1 cup (225 g) unsalted butter

1 ½ cups (150 g) powdered sugar, sifted

1 large egg, at room temperature

2 teaspoons vanilla extract

Red modelling chocolate or fondant

Red luster dust

2 ounces (60 g) dark chocolate, melted

Piping gel

If you're reading this, you're probably the type of person who already knows (and loves?) Krampus. But for those who need a reminder, this terrifying creature is a half-man, half-goat menace that comes around every December and takes away naughty children in his basket, sometimes even dragging them to Hell. This demon-like beast comes from the folklore of Austria's Alpine region and is often depicted with a long snake-like tongue. Kram-puss, however, is my interpretation of Krampus as a cat—a lot less scary, especially in cookie form. To make these cookies, you could use a cat face-shaped cookie cutter, but a silicone mold takes it to another level and is worth the small fee. Search for "cat face silicone mold" online; there are loads of different designs out there!

1. In a large bowl, combine the flour, cocoa powder, and salt and set aside.

2. In the bowl of an electric mixer fitted with the paddle attachment, beat the butter on high speed until light and fluffy, 2 to 3 minutes.

3. Add the powdered sugar and mix on low speed to start. Continue mixing on medium speed until fully incorporated.

4. Add the egg and vanilla and keep mixing. Turn the speed back down to low and add the dry ingredient mixture.

(continued on next page)

(continued from previous page)

5. Divide the dough in two, cover with plastic wrap, and refrigerate for at least two hours.

6. While the dough is chilling, make the tongues. Shape the modelling chocolate or fondant into pointy tongues and leave to dry out, about 45 minutes. Once dry to the touch, brush the tongues with luster dust.

7. Prepare two baking sheets with parchment paper.

8. Take one half of the cookie dough and start molding the cat faces by pressing a small ball of dough into the cat mold (it helps to dust it with a little flour beforehand).

9. Unmold and place the cookies on the baking sheets and freeze for 15 minutes. This ensures they maintain their shape after baking.

10. Preheat the oven to 375°F (190°C).

11. Bake the cookies for 7 to 9 minutes, or until the sides start to brown.

12. Remove from the oven and place on a cooling rack. While the cookies are still warm, make an indentation in the mouth with a sharp knife to make room for the tongue. Leave to cool completely.

13. Add the tongues by dipping the end in the melted chocolate and inserting in the mouth. The tongues will be held in place as the chocolate hardens.

14. Brush the tongues with piping gel to give them a wet look.

Lavender Moon Shortbread

YIELD: 24 cookies ⚜ PREP TIME: 10 minutes, plus overnight chill time ⚜ BAKE TIME: 12 to 14 minutes

3/4 cup (170 g) unsalted butter,
    at room temperature
1/3 cup (80 ml) maple syrup
1/4 cup (55 g) packed light brown sugar
3/4 teaspoon dried lavender buds
1 3/4 cups (220 g) all-purpose flour,
    plus more for rolling
1 tablespoon cornstarch
1/4 teaspoon salt

What's more luscious, dark, and goth than a stroll through a moonlit garden? The only thing that could make it more perfect is a Victorian tea party at the end. This shortbread is the ideal companion to the Lavender Maple Moon Milk on page 151.

1. In the bowl of an electric mixer fitted with the paddle attachment, beat the butter, maple syrup, and brown sugar until light and fluffy.

2. In a separate bowl using a fork, mix the lavender, flour, cornstarch, and salt.

3. Add the dry ingredients to the butter mixture and mix until fully incorporated, making sure to scrape the sides and bottom of the bowl.

4. Cover the dough with plastic wrap and refrigerate for 1 hour or overnight.

5. Preheat the oven to 350°F (175°C) and line two baking sheets with parchment paper.

6. On a floured surface, roll the dough to 1/4-inch (1/2-cm) thickness and cut out crescent moon shapes with a sharp knife (or use a crescent moon–shaped cookie cutter if you have one); each should be about 3 inches (8 cm) tall. Make a slit at the bottom so the cookie can sit on the rim of the mug.

7. Place on the prepared baking sheets and bake for 12 to 14 minutes, or until the edges start to brown.

8. Let cool completely before adding to your mugs of tea, coffee, or moon milk.

Pumpkin Jelly Pops

YIELD: 12 ❧ PREP TIME: 25 minutes ❧ CHILL TIME: Overnight

3 packets powder gelatin
2 cups (400 g) granulated sugar
1 teaspoon pumpkin extract
Orange food coloring
3D pumpkin silicone molds
12 lollipop sticks
½ cup (100 g) superfine sugar
1 tablespoon citric acid

I am fascinated by set design and movie props. There are a handful of films I watch purely for the costume and set design. These movies fill me with inspiration, and it is precisely a film that gave me the idea for these jelly pops. In the first Harry Potter movie there's an amazing scene filmed in the Great Hall during Halloween that includes an array of sweets displayed on the hall tables with cauldrons filled with lollipops and chocolates. While I was able to buy most of the treats featured, I had to make my own 3D pumpkin jellies. You can find the molds online for an affordable price—just search for "3D pumpkin silicone mold."

1. In a large saucepan, add ½ cup (100 ml) of water and sprinkle the gelatin on top. Allow to bloom for 5 minutes.

2. In a separate saucepan, add ¾ cup (180ml) of water over low-medium heat and bring to a boil. Add the granulated sugar and stir until fully dissolved.

3. Pour the sugar mixture into the pan with the gelatin mixture and stir until completely dissolved, then simmer on low heat for 5 minutes.

4. Add the pumpkin extract and enough food coloring to get a good pumpkin-like orange hue.

5. Spray your molds with nonstick spray and carefully pour in the mixture. Add a lollipop stick to each one (it helps to hold them with a clothespin, so they stay in the middle of the mold). Refrigerate overnight.

6. When the jelly is firm, in a shallow bowl or plate, mix the superfine sugar with the citric acid. Unmold and roll the jelly pops in the sugar mixture to fully coat.

Ghoulish Breads and Pastries

Bat Fougasse

YIELD: 2 bat breads ⚱ PREP TIME: 1 to 2 hours ⚱ BAKE TIME: 15 to 20 minutes

4 ⅛ cups (550 g) bread flour,
   plus more for dusting
½ tablespoon sea salt, plus more
   to sprinkle on top
1 tablespoon instant dry yeast
1 ½ cups (350 ml) lukewarm water
   75° to 79°F (24° to 26°C)
2 tablespoons olive oil, plus more
   for brushing
⅓ cup (40 g) poppy seeds

To me, fougasse is the French response to the Italian focaccia. Typically oval-shaped with slits at each side, fougasse calls to mind an autumnal leaf. It is those slits that gave me the idea of a bat wing and consequently a bat-shaped fougasse. I recommend making your favorite dip to go along with your fougasse, and the bread would look adorable presented in a wicker basket.

1. In the bowl of an electric mixer with the hook attachment, mix the flour, salt, and yeast. Add the lukewarm water and olive oil and continue mixing for 5 to 7 minutes.

2. Cover and leave to rise in a warm place until doubled in size, about 1 hour.

3. After the dough has doubled in size, punch it down and turn out onto a floured surface. Divide the dough in half.

4. Using your hands, roll and mold each half into the shape of a bat, using scissors if necessary to define the wings, ears, and feet. Transfer to a piece of parchment paper.

5. With a sharp knife, score the slits on each wing. Cover and leave to rise for 20 minutes.

6. Preheat the oven to 430°F (220°C).

7. Brush the dough bats with olive oil, and sprinkle with salt and the poppy seeds. Bake for 15 to 20 minutes until golden brown. Remove and let cool before serving with your favorite dip.

The Dark Lord's Tower

YIELD: 20 to 25 choux buns ♀ PREP TIME: 30 minutes, plus 3 hours chill time ♀ BAKE TIME: 45 minutes

CRAQUELIN

1/2 cup (115 g) unsalted butter,
    at room temperature
1 cup minus 2 tablespoons (100 g)
    all-purpose flour
2 tablespoons Dutch process cocoa
3/4 cup (165 g) packed dark brown sugar
1 teaspoon vanilla extract
Black gel food coloring (see Note)

CHOUX PASTRY DOUGH

6 1/2 ounces (185 g) all-purpose flour,
    sifted
1 tablespoon superfine sugar
1/2 teaspoon sea salt
1 3/4 cups (450 ml) water
Red gel food coloring
3/4 cup (170 g) unsalted butter
6 large eggs, beaten

WHITE CHOCOLATE
GANACHE FILLING

24 ounces (680 g) white chocolate,
    chopped
1 cup (240 ml) heavy whipping cream
1 teaspoon vanilla extract
Red cocoa-based food coloring

ASSEMBLY

Isomalt, melted, for glueing
10 1/2-inch-tall (27 cm) polystyrene cone

This croquembouche centerpiece is of course inspired by Mount Doom, perfect for Middle-earth fans . . . or any dark lords themselves! Filled with a red-tinted white chocolate ganache and topped with black craquelin, these choux buns give the illusion of volcanic rock. Wouldn't it be a fun way to propose by hiding a ring in one of these smouldering gems?

1. To make the craquelin: In the bowl of an electric mixer fitted with the paddle attachment, beat the butter, flour, cocoa powder, brown sugar, vanilla, and food coloring on medium speed until combined.

2. Spread the dough on a large piece of parchment paper and top with another piece of equal size. Roll out to 1/8-inch (3-mm) thick.

3. Place in the freezer for 1 hour or until ready to use.

4. To make the choux buns: Preheat the oven to 425°F (220°C) and line two baking sheets with parchment paper.

5. In a small bowl, combine the flour, sugar, and salt.

6. In a saucepan, add the water and the red food coloring over medium-low heat. Add the butter and stir until melted. Bring to a quick boil, then stir in the flour mixture all at once with a wooden spoon. Stir vigorously until the dough comes off the sides of the pan and forms a ball.

7. Transfer the dough to an electric mixer fitted with the paddle attachment and beat on low speed for 3 to 4 minutes to cool it down. Start adding the beaten eggs slowly until you get a glossy dough that holds its shape. You may not need to use all the eggs.

8. Spoon the mixture into a large pastry bag with a plain round tip and pipe balls of pastry just over an inch in diameter onto the prepared baking sheets.

9. Remove the craquelin from the freezer and peel off the top piece of parchment. Using a round cutter that is the same or slightly bigger diameter as the balls of choux you just piped, cut out circles of dough. Place a craquelin circle on top of each choux ball.

10. Reduce the oven temperature to 400°F (205°C) and bake the choux buns for 25 to 30 minutes, until they start to brown. Remove from the oven and prick a hole in the base of each bun to release steam.

11. Reduce the oven temperature again to 350°F (175°C) and bake for a further 5 to 8 minutes to dry out.

12. Remove from the oven and leave to cool completely.

13. To make the filling: In a large bowl, combine the white chocolate and cream and warm in the microwave at 30-second intervals stirring in between until melted and combined.

14. Mix in the vanilla and red food coloring and leave the mixture to cool. Cover with plastic wrap, making sure it touches the mixture to prevent air bubbles forming.

15. Refrigerate for 2 hours. Remove and whisk for 2 minutes, or until you reach a smooth, spreadable consistency.

16. Add the ganache to a pastry bag with a small round tip and use the tip to slightly enlarge the hole in the choux buns. Fill them generously with ganache until you see the filling oozing back toward you slightly.

17. To assemble: Using a teaspoon or so of the melted isomalt, attach the polystyrene cone to a serving plate, then assemble by attaching the choux buns in circles dipping in the isomalt first, starting at the bottom and working your way up.

18. Use the remaining ganache to drizzle around the croquembouche making it look like flowing lava.

NOTE | Always make the craquelin first as it takes a while to firm up in the freezer.

Toadstool Dinner Rolls

YIELD: 10 mushrooms ⚲ **PREP TIME:** 1 ½ hours, plus 2 hours and 15 minutes rise time ⚲ **BAKE TIME:** 15 to 16 minutes

ROLL DOUGH

1 cup (240 ml) whole milk
4 tablespoons (60 g) unsalted butter
18 ounces (510 g) bread flour
2 ½ teaspoons fast-acting yeast
2 tablespoons granulated sugar
2 teaspoons sea salt
2 large eggs

MUSHROOM CAP DOUGH

3/4 cup (120 g) rice flour
1 tablespoon fast-acting yeast
1/4 teaspoon sea salt
1 tablespoon superfine sugar
1 tablespoon vegetable oil
Red gel food coloring
1/2 cup (120 ml) warm water,
    105° to 115°F (40° to 46°C)

When you conjure in your mind the image of a mystical, goth toadstool, I guarantee you'll be picturing the amanita muscaria, commonly known as the fly agaric. I could bore you talking about my fascination with this mushroom, but I'll just stick to the recipe! I achieved the cracked top for these buns by using rice flour, just as you would when making tiger bread. You'll also need a cylinder-style pan or silicone mold to achieve the stems. You don't necessarily need to have stems for these, but they definitely add to the magic of these rolls.

1. To make the rolls: In a saucepan, combine the milk and butter. Heat over medium heat until the butter is fully melted. Let the mixture cool down to lukewarm.

2. In the bowl of an electric mixer fitted with the hook attachment, add the flour and yeast to one side of the bowl and the granulated sugar and salt to the other. This is to avoid the salt potentially killing the yeast.

3. Start the mixer on low and slowly add the warm milk and butter mixture. Then add the eggs one at a time.

4. Once fully combined, cover the bowl with a damp tea towel and leave to rise in a warm place for 1 to 1 ½ hours or until doubled in size.

(continued on next page)

(continued from previous page)

5. Turn out the dough, punch it down, and knead a couple of times to knock out the air, then divide the dough into 10 equal pieces. Fill 2 by 2-inch (5 by 5-cm) cylinder molds with the dough. They will be overfilled but that's how the cap of the mushroom is created.

6. Cover and leave in a warm place to rise again for 30 minutes.

7. Meanwhile, make the mushroom cap dough. To an electric mixer with the paddle attachment, add the rice flour. Then add the yeast to one side and the salt to the other side along with the superfine sugar, oil, and food coloring. With the mixer on low speed, start adding the warm water. Mix until everything is combined. Cover and let rest for 15 minutes.

8. Preheat the oven to 425°F (220°C).

9. Using your hands spread the red dough over the cap tops of your roll dough. Make sure the whole top and sides are well covered.

10. Bake for 15 to 16 minutes. Remove from oven and let cool before serving.

Devils' Fingers Pastries

YIELD: 14 to 16 fingers ⚬ PREP TIME: 1 hour, plus 50 minutes chill time ⚬ BAKE TIME: 30 minutes

PASTRY DOUGH

4 ¼ cups (530 g) all-purpose flour,
    plus extra for dusting
2 scant teaspoons sea salt
1 cup plus 2 tablespoons (250 g) cold,
    unsalted butter, cubed
2 large egg yolks
7 to 8 tablespoons ice-cold water
Red gel food coloring

SAUSAGE FILLING

1 pound (455 g) pork sausages
¾ cup (150 g) roasted red peppers,
    drained, patted dry, and chopped
Finely grated zest of one lemon
1 tablespoon tomato purée
½ teaspoon crushed mustard seeds
¼ teaspoon sea salt
¼ teaspoon black pepper

DECORATION

16 whole almonds
Black edible paint
Edible glue

Inspired by the traditional witch finger cookies, these devils' fingers are savory, filled with a delicious sausage meat mixture. To make them hollow, I have used cream horn molds, but you can also make a cone out of cardboard covered in aluminum foil to wrap the pastry around. If you don't have cardboard, a triple layer of aluminum foil will be sturdy enough to hold the pastry wrap.

1. To make the pastry dough: On a clean surface, combine the flour and salt. Add the butter and rub it between your fingers until it resembles breadcrumbs or use a food processor to combine.

2. Make a well in the center of the mixture and add the egg yolks, water, and food coloring. You may not need all the water, and you should continue to add as much of the food coloring as you need to get to your desired red color. Mix by hand and bring the dough together to form a smooth ball. Wrap in plastic wrap and refrigerate for 30 minutes.

3. Meanwhile, make the filling. Cut the sausages lengthwise, remove the meat from the casings, and add to a mixing bowl. Add the peppers, lemon zest, tomato purée, and mustard seeds. Season with the salt and pepper and mix well with your hands.

(continued on next page)

(continued from previous page)

4. Remove the dough from the refrigerator. Take off the plastic wrap and cut a piece of dough big enough to wrap around your mold. Shape into a cone making sure it isn't too thick as you will be filling them.

5. Using your own finger as reference, shape the dough by pinching the top third and underneath knuckle to shape it like a finger, then make some slits with a knife. Using an almond, make a dent where the fingernail will be placed.

6. Repeat until all the dough is used. Place your molds on a tray lined with parchment paper and refrigerate for 20 minutes.

7. Preheat the oven to 350°F (175°C).

8. Take your tray from the refrigerator and put directly into the oven. Bake for 15 minutes. Let the fingers cool slightly, then remove the molds and fill the pastry with the sausage mixture using a pastry bag.

9. Return to the oven and bake for another 14 minutes.

10. While the fingers are baking, paint all the almond nails with black edible paint and let dry.

11. Remove the fingers from the oven and cool completely before attaching the nails with edible glue.

NOTE | For added effect, after filling the fingers with the sausage mixture, add a layer of ketchup in the middle using another pastry bag. When you cut the fingers in half, the ketchup mimics blood.

TIP | To make this recipe vegan, use store-bought vegan pastry and fill with a creamy filling made with your choice of mushrooms, white onions, garlic, white wine, and vegan cream.

Wild Mushroom and Potato Ouija Pie

YIELD: Serves 8 ♀ PREP TIME: 1 hour and 10 minutes, plus 30 minutes chill time ♀ BAKE TIME: 30 to 35 minutes

PASTRY DOUGH

3 1/3 cups (415 g) all-purpose flour
2 scant teaspoons sea salt
1 cup plus 2 tablespoons (250 g)
    unsalted butter, cold and cubed
3 large egg yolks, divided
3 1/2 fluid ounces (100 ml)
    ice cold water

MUSHROOM FILLING

4 tablespoons (55 g) unsalted butter
6 large shallots, finely chopped
1 pound (450 g) mushrooms,
    roughly chopped
2 cups (480 ml) chicken broth
1 tablespoon soy sauce
1 tablespoon smoked paprika
2 teaspoons dried dill
3 tablespoons all-purpose flour
1 cup (240 ml) whole milk
1/2 cup (123 g) sour cream
Half a lemon, juiced
Sea salt and black pepper, to taste

POTATO TOPPING

2 large potatoes, thinly sliced

I made this ghoulish mushroom and potato pie for my fellow bakers during a little reunion we had after Christmas last year. I completely made it up at the time, but it was such a success that I would absolutely stock it in my little gothic bakeshop. I used to only eat wild mushrooms when I was able to forage them, but nowadays more and more species of mushrooms are being cultivated and are readily available in most supermarkets. I recommend you make the pastry from scratch as store-bought pastry contains a lot of water and reduces in size during the baking.

1. To make the pastry: On a clean surface, combine the flour and salt. Add the butter and rub it between your fingers until it resembles breadcrumbs. Alternatively, you can use a food processor for this.

2. Make a well in the center and add 2 of the egg yolks and the cold water. Mix with your hands and bring the dough together to form a smooth ball. Wrap in plastic wrap and refrigerate for 30 minutes.

3. While the pastry chills, make the filling. In a large saucepan, melt the butter over medium heat. Add the shallots and cook for 5 minutes. Add the mushrooms and cook for 5 more minutes. Stir in the broth, soy sauce, paprika, and dill. Reduce the heat to low, cover, and simmer for 15 minutes.

(continued on next page)

(continued from previous page)

4. Sprinkle the flour into the pan and mix well. Add the milk, mix again, cover, and simmer for another 15 minutes stirring occasionally.

5. Add the sour cream, lemon juice, and season with salt and pepper. Pour into your chosen baking dish (see Tip).

6. To prepare the topping: Preheat the oven to 356°F (180°C). In a medium saucepan, parboil the potatoes over medium heat for 10 minutes in salted boiling water. Carefully remove and pat dry. Add to a roasting pan and roast for 30 to 35 minutes, until golden brown.

7. Top the mushroom filling with a layer of potatoes. Set aside.

8. Remove the pastry dough from the fridge. On a lightly floured surface, roll your pastry to ¼-inch (½-cm) thickness. Put your baking dish on top of the pastry and use it as a guide to cut out an equal sized portion. Place the pastry on top of the potatoes in the dish.

9. Decorate by using any leftover dough to cut letters, numbers, and additional shapes (for example flowers, leaves, suns, moons) with cookie cutters or freehand with a knife, and arrange as you like. Beat the remaining egg yolk and use it to secure the dough pieces.

10. Preheat the oven to 350°F (175°C). Brush the remaining egg wash all over the pie top and bake for 30 to 35 minutes, or until the pastry is golden brown.

NOTE | I used a mushroom blend of chestnut, oyster, and shiitake, but you can use any you like.

TIPS | If using a large baking dish (approximately 9 by 13 inches, 23 by 34 cm), double the filling recipe. If you are using a smaller dish, then leave the quantities as they are.

You can make shapes for your decoration using silicone molds. Just press the dough inside the mold and gently remove when ready.

Horror Clown Potato Bread Rolls

YIELD: 12 clowns | PREP TIME: 2 hours, plus 2 hours rise time | BAKE TIME: 40 to 45 minutes

POTATO DOUGH

½ pound (225 g) potatoes,
    peeled and chopped (see Note)
2 ½ teaspoons fast-acting yeast
¼ cup (60 ml) lukewarm water
½ cup (115 g) unsalted butter,
    melted and divided, plus extra for
    greasing the pan
1 large bunch fresh chives,
    finely chopped (optional)
2 tablespoons granulated sugar
2 teaspoons sea salt
14 ounces (400 g) bread flour

DECORATION

Red, black, and white edible ink pens

These potato bread rolls made me very popular when I was a university student. Every time I made them, they practically flew out of the pan! The potato content makes them fluffy and delicious. Turning them into famous horror clowns is the icing on the bun! The clowns featured are Pennywise from *It*, Billy from *Saw*, Joker, and clowns from *House of 1000 Corpses*, *Killer Clowns from Outer Space*, and *Clownhouse*. Choose to make any that you like (or hate)!

1. To make the dough: In a medium pan, add the potatoes and cover with cold water. Bring to a boil over medium-high heat then reduce the heat to low, and simmer 15 to 20 minutes, until tender.

2. Drain, reserving 1 cup (250 ml) of liquid, and mash with a potato masher. Let the potatoes cool until lukewarm.

3. In a small bowl, sprinkle the yeast over the lukewarm water and let stand for 5 minutes.

4. In the bowl of an electric mixer fitted with the hook attachment, add the reserved potato liquid, the mashed potato, dissolved yeast, and half the melted butter. Add the chives, sugar, and salt. Mix on low speed until combined.

(continued on next page)

(continued from previous page)

5. Stir in the flour bit by bit until it is fully incorporated. The dough will be sticky. Continue mixing for about 5 minutes until the dough becomes smooth.

6. Cover the bowl and leave to rise in a warm place for 1 to 1 $1/2$ hours, or until doubled in size.

7. Turn out the dough on a clean surface and knock the air out of the dough by punching down and kneading for a few seconds. Divide into 13 equal balls. (One of them will be used for noses and cheeks.)

8. Brush a 9 by 13-inch baking dish with melted butter and place 12 balls in 3 rows of 4. Add little ball noses and cheeks to some of them using the 13th ball of dough.

9. Brush the dough balls with the remaining melted butter until all is used. Cover with a clean tea towel and leave to do a second rise for 30 to 40 minutes.

10. Preheat the oven to 375°F (190°C). Bake for 40 to 45 minutes, or until golden brown. Allow to cool completely before decorating.

11. To decorate: Use reference images of your chosen horror clowns to draw their standout makeup features with the edible ink pens. Use additional colors if necessary.

NOTES

The potatoes only need to be broken down slightly, about two or three pieces. Just small enough that they can fit into your pot and be covered with the water. And you can use any kind you like!

The chives are optional, but they do add to the layers of flavor in the rolls.

Spiderweb Galette des Rois

YIELD: Serves 8 ⚱ PREP TIME: 15 minutes, plus 30 minutes chill time ⚱ BAKE TIME: 25 to 30 minutes

½ cup (115 g) salted butter, softened
½ cup (100 g) superfine sugar
1 cup (115 g) almond flour
Zest of ½ orange
2 tablespoons cognac
Pinch fine sea salt
1 pound (450 g) puff pastry
Apricot jam
1 large egg, beaten

Galette des rois is eaten mainly in France on the feast of the Epiphany, the Twelfth Night of Christmas. In Spain we have a similar tradition of eating roscón de reyes on January 6th. These "kings cakes" have figurines hidden inside, and whoever gets one in their slice must bring the cake the following year. Galette des rois is quite simple to make: puff pastry filled with frangipane and decorated with geometric lines. And that's where the spooky version comes in—we are going to score it with a spiderweb design instead!

1. In a large bowl, mix together the softened butter and sugar until light and fluffy. You can use an electric mixer if you want, but I tend to do this by hand with a wooden spoon or spatula.

2. Add the almond flour, orange zest, cognac, and salt and continue mixing until it all comes together.

3. Line a baking sheet with parchment paper. Set aside.

4. Roll out half the puff pastry on a lightly floured surface and cut a 10-inch (25-cm) circle using a plate or a pot lid as template. Repeat with the remaining pastry.

5. Place one circle of pastry on the prepared baking sheet, and brush lightly with apricot jam leaving a ¾-inch (2-cm) gap at the edge.

6. Spread or pipe the almond mixture evenly over the jam, then cover with the second circle of pastry.

7. Press the edges to seal. You can dampen your fingers with a little water to help the sealing process.

8. Refrigerate for 30 minutes.

9. Preheat the oven to 375°F (190°C).

10. Remove the galette from the refrigerator and score a spiderweb design on top using a sharp knife.

11. Brush with the beaten egg and bake for 25 to 30 minutes, or until golden brown.

TIP If you prefer, you can use ground almonds in place of almond flour and rum instead of cognac.

Batty Scones

YIELD: 6 bats ♀ PREP TIME: 30 minutes ♀ BAKE TIME: 15 to 20 minutes

SCONE DOUGH

2 cups (250 g) all-purpose flour
¾ cup (170 g) unsalted butter,
    cold, cut into cubes
2 teaspoons baking powder
2 teaspoons cocoa powder
Black food coloring
¾ cup (150 g) superfine sugar
¾ cup (175 g) mixed dried fruit
1 teaspoon ground cinnamon
¼ teaspoon fresh nutmeg, grated
Pinch sea salt
Zest of 1 large orange
2 large eggs, beaten
1 to 2 tablespoons whole milk

DECORATION

6 glacé cherries, halved
12 blanched almonds
Clear isomalt
Black gel food coloring

These treats are the vampire equivalent to fat rascals, a scone-like baked good traditional to Yorkshire where I live. Although it was the iconic Yorkshire-based tearoom Betty's that made the fat rascals popular, the recipe goes back to the fifteenth century. The fat rascal's predecessor was the turf bun, so called because they were cooked on a griddle over a turf fire at the end of the cooking day. Leftover bits of lard-based dough were mixed in with dried fruits and honey, flattened, and cooked. Today's fat rascal is characterized by having glacé cherry "eyes" and almond "teeth," practically a little vampire already! For my version (originally called Bat Rascals as a play on the fat rascals from my beloved Betty's, however I thought better to change up the name just in case the tearoom gets funny with me) we are going to color them a spooky gray-black, sharpen those almond teeth into fangs, and attach some little isomalt bat wings.

(continued on next page)

(continued from previous page)

1. Preheat the oven to 350°F (175°C) and line a large baking sheet with parchment paper or a silicone mat.

2. To make the dough: In a food processor, add the flour and butter and pulse until you have a breadcrumb-like texture. Alternatively, rub the butter and flour with your fingertips.

3. Add the baking powder, cocoa, food coloring, sugar, dried fruit, cinnamon, nutmeg, salt, and orange zest and pulse a few more times until all ingredients are combined. Do not overmix.

4. In a large bowl, combine the mixture with 1 $\frac{1}{2}$ tablespoons of the beaten egg. The mixture should be moist enough to hold its shape and not overly dry or crumbly. If it is too dry, add the 1 to 2 tablespoons of milk.

5. Divide the dough into six equal pieces. Shape each piece into a round cookie shape 1 to 1 $\frac{1}{2}$ inches (3 to 4 cm) thick. Place the cookies on the baking sheet and glaze with the remaining beaten egg.

6. To decorate: Place two cherry halves on top to look like eyes and carve the blanched almonds to look like fangs. Press them onto the mouth area.

7. Bake for 15 to 20 minutes. Once the rascals are out of the oven and cooled, they should sound hollow like bread rolls when tapped at the bottom.

8. Draw the shape of a bat wing onto a piece of paper and place some parchment paper on top making sure you can see through it.

9. Melt the isomalt in the microwave following the manufacturer's instructions. Add the food coloring and stir with a spatula.

10. Spoon the isomalt over the bat shape and let it set. Peel off, then turn the drawing over and do the same for the other side wing.

11. Repeat the process until you have all the wings. Stick the wings to the sides of the rascals with a little melted isomalt.

NOTE | When making your wings, the method above will yield a very rustic design. For a more polished look, use a silicone mold in the wing style of your choosing and pour the isomalt in.

TIP | If you want your bat's teeth to be really prominent (or if you find carving regular blanched almonds too challenging due to their size) swap for marcona almonds, which are larger.

Steam-Pump(kin) Bao Buns

YIELD: 10 to 12 buns ❖ PREP TIME: 30 minutes, plus 1 hour 15 minutes rise time ❖ BAKE TIME: 12 to 14 minutes

BUN DOUGH

2 teaspoons active dry yeast

2 tablespoons granulated sugar

1/2 cup plus 2 tablespoons (150 ml) warm water, approximately 110°F (43°C)

2 1/2 cups (315 g) all-purpose flour

1/2 teaspoon baking powder

1/2 teaspoon baking soda

2 teaspoons sea salt

1/4 cup (60 ml) vegetable oil

Green food coloring

Orange food coloring

PORK FILLING

1 pound (450 g) ground pork

1/2 teaspoon sea salt

1/2 teaspoon white pepper

1 cup finely chopped chives

1 large clove garlic, finely chopped

1 teaspoon finely chopped fresh ginger

1 teaspoon sesame oil

2 teaspoons soy sauce

DIPPING SAUCE

2 tablespoons soy sauce

2 teaspoons rice wine vinegar

2 teaspoons sesame oil

Chili flakes, to taste

Forty 14-inch-long pieces of kitchen twine, soaked in vegetable oil

I'm giving a little autumnal twist to these traditional Chinese bao buns. I've chosen a savory filling, but this recipe is versatile and can easily be made sweet too. To give even more dimension to these beauties, I like to paint a little green around the stem of the pumpkin with food coloring. They're visually stunning! I can imagine displaying these in dark wicker baskets behind the counter of my little gothic bakeshop and serving them in beautiful carboard boxes wrapped with ribbons and sealed with a wax stamp.

(continued on next page)

(continued from previous page)

1. To make the dough: In a small bowl, combine the yeast, sugar, and warm water and leave for 5 minutes to bubble.

2. In the bowl of an electric mixer fitted with the hook attachment, combine the flour, baking powder, baking soda, and salt. Add the yeast mixture and the oil and knead for around 5 minutes, or until the dough comes together. Add a little more water if the dough looks dry.

3. Pinch about a large tablespoon of dough and place in a small bowl with the green food coloring. Mix until fully combined, cover with plastic wrap and set aside to rise for 45 minutes.

4. To the remaining dough, add the orange food coloring and mix until fully incorporated. Cover with a damp tea towel and leave to rest alongside the green dough. This is not a traditional bread dough, so it won't rise as much.

5. Once the rise is complete, punch the doughs to deflate and knead a couple of times. Then cover and let rest for another 30 minutes.

6. Meanwhile, make the filling. In a large bowl, combine the pork, salt, pepper, chives, garlic, ginger, sesame oil, and soy sauce. Mix with gloved hands or a wooden spoon until fully incorporated.

7. After the second rise, divide the orange dough into 10 to 12 equal pieces. Roll each piece into a 4-inch (10-cm) circle. Add a large tablespoon of filling in the center of each circle and bring the edges together to form a ball.

8. Place two pieces of twine on your countertop making a cross and then the other two placed diagonally, like the beginning of a spiderweb. Place a filled dough ball in the center, sealed side down. Tie the twine loosely, one strand at a time with a double knot. Repeat with the remaining dumplings and twine.

9. Make the stems with the green dough by rolling each one into a 3-inch rope, and then curling them around a toothpick.

10. Place each pumpkin in a square piece of parchment paper and steam for 12 to 14 minutes in a steamer basket over a pan of boiling water. Make sure the pumpkins don't touch each other by cooking in batches.

11. Place the stems on top of each pumpkin halfway through the steaming process.

12. Meanwhile, make the dipping sauce. In a small bowl, add the soy sauce, vinegar, sesame oil, and chili flakes. Mix until well combined.

13. Once the buns are done, remove the toothpicks, twine, and parchment paper. Allow to cool slightly and serve with the dipping sauce.

Black Widow Profiteroles

YIELD: 15 spiders ⚬ PREP TIME: 1 hour, plus 1 hour chill time ⚬ BAKE TIME: 45 minutes

CRAQUELIN

1/2 cup (115 g) unsalted butter, softened
1 cup minus 2 tablespoons (100 g) all-purpose flour
1 heaping tablespoon cocoa powder
3/4 cup (165 g) packed dark brown sugar
1 teaspoon vanilla extract
Black gel food coloring

CHOUX PASTRY DOUGH

1 1/2 cups (190 g) all-purpose flour, sifted
1 tablespoon superfine sugar
1 tablespoon cocoa powder
1/2 teaspoon sea salt
Black food coloring
3/4 cup (170 g) unsalted butter
6 large eggs, beaten

CARAMEL FILLING

1 can (13.4-ounce, or 380 g) caramel or dulce de leche
Red food coloring

DECORATION

1 bar (3 1/2 ounces, or 100 g) Lindt chocolate, 70 percent cocoa, chopped
Black oil-based food coloring
Handful red candy melts

This is a fun variation of The Dark Lord's Tower croquembouche (page 48). Although the basic recipe for the choux buns remains the same, the way it's presented is completely different. For the filling I've chosen caramel mixed with red food coloring for that oozing blood-like consistency we all enjoy.

1. To make the craquelin: In the bowl of an electric mixer fitted with the paddle attachment, beat the butter, flour, cocoa powder, brown sugar, vanilla, and food coloring on medium speed until combined.

2. Spread the dough on a large piece of parchment paper and top with another piece of parchment of equal size. Roll out to 1/8-inch (3-mm) thick.

3. Place in the freezer for 1 hour or until ready to use.

4. Preheat the oven to 425°F (220°C) and line two baking sheets with parchment paper.

5. To make the choux buns: In a small bowl, combine the flour, sugar, cocoa powder, and salt together.

(continued on next page)

(continued from previous page)

6. In a saucepan, add 1 ¾ cups (450 ml) of water and the black food coloring and set over low-medium heat. Add the butter and stir until melted. Bring to a quick boil, then stir in the flour mixture all at once with a wooden spoon. Stir vigorously until the dough comes off the sides of the pan and forms a ball.

7. Transfer the dough to an electric mixer fitted with the paddle attachment and beat on low speed for 3 to 4 minutes to cool it down. Slowly add the beaten eggs until you get a glossy dough that holds its shape. You may not need to use all the eggs.

8. Spoon the mixture into a large pastry bag with a large round nozzle and pipe balls of pastry around 1-inch (3-cm) diameter onto one of the prepared baking sheets and ½-inch (1.5-cm) diameter onto the other baking sheet.

9. Remove the craquelin from the freezer and peel off the top piece of parchment. Using two round cutters the same diameters as the balls of choux you just piped, cut out circles of dough. Place one on top of each choux ball, matching up the sizes.

10. Reduce the oven temperature to 400°F (205°C) and bake for 25 to 30 minutes, until they start to brown (the smaller sized profiteroles may take a few minutes less to cook). Remove from the oven and prick a hole in the base of each one to release steam.

11. Reduce the oven temperature again to 350°F (175°C) and bake the choux buns for 5 to 8 minutes to dry out.

12. Remove from the oven and leave to cool completely.

13. To make the filling: In a small bowl, mix the caramel with the red food coloring.

14. Spoon into a pastry bag with a metal nozzle and fill the profiteroles with the caramel. Set aside.

15. To decorate: In a microwave-safe bowl, melt the chocolate bar in the microwave at 30-second intervals, stirring in between. Add the food coloring until you get an almost black shade.

16. Add the melted chocolate to a pastry bag and pipe the spider legs and pincers onto a silicone mat (the length of these will vary based on the size of your profiteroles). Once they are fully set, peel them off, turn them around and pipe the opposite side to give them more of a 3D shape and sturdiness.

17. Stick the large and small profiteroles to each other with a little melted chocolate. Then attach the legs (to the larger piece) and pincers (to the smaller piece) the same way.

18. In a microwave-safe bowl, melt the red candy melts at 30-second intervals, stirring in between. Add to a pastry bag and pipe the three red markings, characteristic of the black widow, onto the body.

Apple S-Pies

YIELD: 6 pies ❦ PREP TIME: 20 minutes, plus 10 minutes chill time ❦ BAKE TIME: 15 to 20 minutes

HAND PIE PASTRY

2 ½ cups (315 g) all-purpose flour
½ teaspoon sea salt
1 teaspoon powdered sugar
1 cup (225 g) unsalted butter,
    cut into cubes
4 to 5 tablespoons ice cold water
1 large egg yolk, beaten, for brushing

APPLE FILLING

2 Granny Smith apples, peeled, cored
    and cut into small chunks
¼ cup (55 g) packed brown sugar
1 teaspoon ground cinnamon
¼ teaspoon grated fresh nutmeg
Pinch sea salt
2 tablespoons unsalted butter
1 tablespoon cornstarch

DECORATION

3 seedless green grapes,
    cut in half lengthwise
Black edible paint

Hand pies in America are akin to pasties in the UK. They are treats that can be eaten out of hand, no wrappings necessary, as the fillings are securely encased in pastry. In the past these were particularly handy (pun intended) for laboring workers who needed a quick and easy lunch, but today we enjoy them for their convenience. My version of apple hand pies has mysterious cat eyes made out of grapes, with a super-flaky pastry and an apple-cinnamon filling oozing nostalgia.

1. To make the pastry: In a food processor, add the flour, salt, and powdered sugar and pulse a couple of times to mix it fully.

2. Add the cubed butter and pulse until the mixture resembles breadcrumbs. Alternatively, you can do this with your hands.

3. Add the cold water, 1 tablespoon at a time, until the mixture forms large clumps and holds together when you press it in your hand.

4. Tip the dough onto a clean surface and knead a couple of times to bring it together. Form a ball, flatten, cover with plastic wrap, and refrigerate.

(continued on next page)

(continued from previous page)

5. Meanwhile, make the filling. In a medium-size pan, combine the apples, brown sugar, cinnamon, nutmeg, salt, and butter and cook over medium heat for 6 to 8 minutes, until the apples begin to soften. Add the cornstarch, mix to combine well, and set aside to cool.

6. Remove the pastry dough from the refrigerator and roll on a lightly floured surface to a ¼-inch (½-cm) thickness. Cut out 12 apple shapes using a 4-inch apple-shaped cookie cutter. Keep the leftover pastry.

7. Spoon a couple of teaspoons of the cooled apple mixture into the middle of six of the apple cutouts, leaving ⅓ inch (1 cm) around the edges. Top with the remaining apple cutouts and crimp the edges sealed with a fork.

8. To decorate: Make a dent with the back of a tablespoon in the middle of each pie where the eye will be placed.

9. Add half a grape in each well, cut side up. Then roll out the leftover pastry to a ⅛-inch (3-mm) thickness and cut 6 small circles that cover the width of the grape. Cut the circles in half and place over the grape as top and bottom eyelids. You can also roll little tubes of pastry and place on top of the eyelids to give them "wrinkles."

10. Preheat the oven to 350°F (175°C) and line a baking sheet with parchment paper.

11. Make a few slits underneath the eye to let the steam out and brush each pie fully with the beaten egg yolk.

12. Bake for 15 to 20 minutes, or until golden brown. Let the pies cool completely before painting the cat eye iris with black edible paint.

NOTE | Cutting and placing the grapes lengthwise is key. The natural veining inside will look like the thin iris of a cat's eye and can also serve as a template for tracing with the edible paint.

TIPS | You can swap in other varieties of apples for this recipe. Just make sure they are appropriate for baking—firm, crisp, and slightly tart.

Use a whole grape as a template for the circles of pastry that will become the eyelids. Run your knife around the outside on top of the leftover pastry to trace the approximate size you'll need.

Flying Broomstick Foccacia Muffins

YIELD: 12 muffins ❖ PREP TIME: 30 minutes, plus 2 hours rise time ❖ BAKE TIME: 15 to 20 minutes

FOCACCIA DOUGH

1/2 cup (120 ml) extra-virgin olive oil

2 garlic cloves, finely minced

1 1/2 tablespoons chopped
    fresh rosemary

1/4 teaspoon ground black pepper

2 1/2 cups (340 g) bread flour

2 1/4 teaspoons instant dry yeast

1 teaspoon sea salt, plus
    more for sprinkling

1 cup (240 ml) lukewarm water,
    110° to 115°F (43° to 46°C)

DECORATION

12 fresh rosemary sprigs

1 yellow pepper

Navy blue food coloring

Focaccia must be one of the easiest and tastiest breads to make. I'm going for the classic garlic and rosemary flavors here, especially since the rosemary easily turns into a broomstick!

1. To make the dough: In a small pot, combine the olive oil, garlic, rosemary, and black pepper and warm up over low heat for 6 to 8 minutes, just long enough to infuse the oil. Remove from the heat and let the oil cool slightly.

2. In the bowl of an electric mixer fitted with the hook attachment, mix together the flour, yeast, and 1 teaspoon of the salt on low speed. Slowly add the water and 1/4 cup of the infused oil. Turn the speed up to medium-high and knead for 5 minutes, or until smooth.

3. Cover the bowl with a damp towel or with plastic wrap and leave to rise in a warm place for 1 to 1 1/2 hours, or until doubled in size.

4. Preheat the oven to 450°F (230°C) and brush some of the remaining infused oil on a 12-hole muffin pan.

5. On a clean surface, turn out the dough and punch down. Divide the dough equally into 12 pieces and place in the muffin holes. Gently press into each cavity. Drizzle the last of the infused oil over the dough pieces.

6. Cover and leave to rise for another 30 minutes.

7. To decorate: Prepare the rosemary broomsticks by removing two-thirds of the leaves of each rosemary sprig, using some of those leaves to make the bristles thicker as you place atop each dough piece.

8. Cut stars out of the yellow pepper using a small star cookie cutter and add around the broomstick.

9. In a small bowl, mix the navy blue food coloring with sea salt until all is covered. Sprinkle on top of each muffin. Bake for 15 to 20 minutes.

To-Die-For Desserts

Key Slime Pie

YIELD: Serves 8 ❧ PREP TIME: 30 minutes, plus 1 hour chill time ❧ BAKE TIME: 25 minutes

DARK CHOCOLATE CRUST

22 chocolate sandwich cookies
5 tablespoons salted butter, melted

LIME FILLING

1 (14-ounce, 397-g) can sweetened
    condensed milk
5 large egg yolks
¾ cup (180 ml) fresh lime juice,
    strained
1 tablespoon fresh lime zest
Pinch sea salt
1 teaspoon vanilla extract
Neon green food coloring

MERINGUE

5 large egg whites
5 tablespoons superfine sugar
Neon green food coloring

This key *slime* pie has no season. It can be made year-round, and it should be, since it is such a simple recipe and so very delicious. Adding the neon coloring into the filling and swirling it in the meringue topping along with making the crust with dark chocolate biscuits gives this pie an eerie look, one that is alluring to us all!

1. Preheat the oven to 350°F (175°C).

2. To make the crust: In a food processor, break the sandwich cookies (filling included) and pulse until you get a fine breadcrumb consistency. Add the melted butter and mix until fully incorporated.

3. Press into and up the sides of a 9-inch (23-cm) round pan using your fingers or a flat-bottom cup. Bake for 8 to 10 minutes. Cool completely before filling.

4. To make the filling: In a medium bowl, combine the condensed milk, egg yolks, lime juice and zest, salt, and vanilla. Add the food coloring until you get a vibrant green.

5. Add the filling to the pie crust, smooth the top, and bake for 15 to 18 minutes, or until the filling is just set but still wobbly in the middle. Remove from the oven and let it cool completely, then refrigerate for 1 hour.

6. To make the meringue: In a stand mixer, whip the egg whites until stiff peaks form, adding 1 tablespoon of sugar at a time as to not deflate the meringue. Swirl in some neon green coloring, but do not incorporate it completely; we want to give the illusion of flames!

7. Remove the pie from the refrigerator, top with the meringue, and use a blowtorch to slightly brown it. If you don't have a blowtorch, you can brown the pie in the oven under the broiler for a few minutes.

Mini Pavlovas of Peril

YIELD: 4 pavlovas ◊ PREP TIME: 20 minutes ◊ BAKE TIME: 2 hours and 15 minutes

MERINGUE SHELLS

4 large egg whites
1 cup (200 g) superfine sugar
1 teaspoon vanilla extract
1 teaspoon cornstarch

DECORATION

Royal icing
Red food coloring

WHIPPED CREAM FRUIT FILLING

1 cup heavy whipping cream
2 tablespoons powdered sugar
1 teaspoon vanilla extract
Fresh forest fruits such as strawberries,
    raspberries, blackberries, and
    blueberries

This recipe is for my mum who absolutely loves pavlovas. Meringue shells filled with whipped cream and topped with fresh fruits make for a perfect Summerween barbeque dessert. But beware—those outer shells bite! You've been warned.

1. Preheat the oven to 200°F (90°C).

2. To make the meringue shells: In a stand mixer, whisk the egg whites until stiff peaks form, adding the sugar 1 tablespoon at a time as to not deflate the meringue. Then add the vanilla and cornstarch and keep on mixing until fully combined.

3. Add the meringue to a large pastry bag fitted with a 1/3-inch (1-cm) round piping tip.

4. Turn eight 2 1/2-inch (6.7-cm) semicircle silicone molds (see Note) upside down and pipe 8 shells. Start with a horizontal line of meringue at the base of the semicircle and then one long vertical line in the middle. Fill in the rest at each side.

5. Place the molds on a baking sheet and bake the shells in the oven for 2 hours and 15 minutes. Once cooked, turn off the oven and leave the meringues inside without opening the door until the oven has cooled completely.

(continued on next page)

(continued from previous page)

6. To decorate: Gently remove the shells from the molds. Pipe teeth on the top and bottom shells with the royal icing and let them dry completely.

7. Meanwhile, make the whipped cream. In a stand mixer with the whisk attachment, whip the cream until soft peaks form. Add the sugar and vanilla and continue whipping until cream firms up enough to be scooped.

8. Fill the bottom shell with the whipped cream, then top with your chosen fruits. Add the top shell.

9. Finish decorating by dripping some red food coloring off the teeth to make the pavlovas look more menacing.

NOTE | The suggested mold used in this recipe is the same kind that is used to make hot chocolate bombs. But you can also use good ol' cupcake silicone molds, or simply freehand pipe the shells flat on a baking sheet lined with parchment paper. In the end you should have shapes that resemble the tops and bottoms of giant clams.

TIP | You could make the shells in the evening and leave them to cool overnight in the oven.

Stone Circle Trifle

YIELD: Serves 10 to 12 ⚲ PREP TIME: 30 minutes

EDIBLE STANDING STONES

1 cup (165 g) white chocolate chips
⅓ cup (75 ml) sweetened
    condensed milk
3 to 4 chocolate sandwich cookies,
    crushed
Black food coloring

EARTH TRIFLE LAYERS

2 cups (360g) candy-coated
    chocolate rocks or pebbles
1 cup (28 g) pretzels
1 cup (100 g) crumbled graham crackers
2 cups (480 ml) ready-made
    chocolate pudding
14 ounces (400 g) store-bought
    brownies, crumbled
3 tablespoons freshly brewed coffee
3 tablespoons Irish cream liqueur
1 cup (240 ml) whipping cream
2 cups (134 g) crumbled store-bought
    icing-free yellow cake
Mossy-green food coloring

This dessert is inspired by one of my favorite stone circles in the UK. It isn't as impressive as Stonehenge, but its setting is peaceful, and it is 700 years older—the Castlerigg Stone Circle in the Lake District. For this trifle I wanted to expose the Earth's layers, topping them with edible moss and cookies and cream standing stones. It looks impressive, but it isn't that much work. My secret? Almost every ingredient is store-bought to create an accessible recipe that will be easy for you to recreate at home.

1. To make the standing stones: Using a double boiler, melt the white chocolate and condensed milk in a heat-proof bowl. Remove from the heat and mix in the crushed cookies and a few drops of the black food coloring. Mix and let rest for 5 minutes.

2. Shape the standing stones onto parchment paper. They can be irregular, with each having a unique size and shape. Let them sit to firm up; the stones won't harden completely as they will be of a fudge consistency.

3. To make the trifle: Make the first layer by pouring the edible rocks into a trifle dish. This layer should be about an inch thick.

(continued on next page)

(continued from previous page)

4. In a food processor, crumble the pretzels and graham crackers and add on top of the rocks. This will create a sand-like layer.

5. Add half the chocolate pudding to create the next layer. In a small bowl, mix together the crumbled brownies, coffee, and Irish cream liqueur. Layer on top of the pudding, then add the other half of the pudding.

6. In a stand mixer, whip the cream until soft peaks form, and color with the moss-green food coloring. Layer on top of the custard.

7. In a small bowl, mix in more moss green color with the cake crumbs and add to the dish for the next layer.

8. Finally, top with the edible standing stones, sticking each one upright around the rim of the trifle dish, with a few standing tall in the middle as well.

TIPS

Looking to up the spooky factor? Add some chocolate bones between the trifle layers to really make this recipe scream.

If you're not finding the mossy shade of green you want, you can add brown food coloring to green a little at a time until you achieve your desired shade.

Gothic Arch
Peanut Butter Cheesecake

YIELD: Serves 10 to 12 ⚱ PREP TIME: 30 minutes, plus 6 hours or overnight chill time ⚱ BAKE TIME: 8 to 10 minutes

COOKIE CRUST

24 chocolate sandwich cookies
4 tablespoons (55 g) salted butter,
    melted

CHEESECAKE FILLING

2 ¼ cups (500 g) cream cheese,
    at room temperature
1 ¾ cups (220 g) powdered sugar
1 teaspoon vanilla extract
1 cup (240 ml) smooth peanut butter
½ cup (120 ml) heavy cream

GANACHE TOPPING

1 cup (240 ml) heavy cream
1 ½ cups (260 g) semi-sweet
    chocolate chips

DECORATION

1 cup (175 g) semi-sweet chocolate chips
Dark fruits, such as blackberries
    and blueberries
Edible purple flowers
Mint leaves
White, milk, and dark chocolate skulls

The kind of cheesecake that could easily be served at Count Dracula's wedding, the piped chocolate Gothic arches are what give this dessert that eerie, romantic look. Combined with the dark fruits and the edible skulls, this is the ultimate gothic treat. Research your favorite Gothic arches online to use as templates!

1. Preheat the oven to 350°F (175°C).

2. To make the crust: In a food processor, add the chocolate sandwich cookies (filling included) and pulse until they resemble breadcrumbs. Add the melted butter and mix until combined.

3. Press the mixture into the bottom and up the sides of a 6-inch (15-cm) springform pan.

4. Bake for 8 to 10 minutes. Set aside to cool completely.

5. To make the filling: In a stand mixer, combine the cream cheese, sugar, vanilla, peanut butter, and heavy cream and mix until smooth. Pour into the cooled crust and refrigerate for 6 hours or overnight.

(continued on next page)

(continued from previous page)

6. To make the ganache: In a saucepan, warm up the cream to just before boiling. Add the chocolate chips to a heatproof bowl then pour the cream over them. Leave for a few minutes then mix well with a spatula.

7. Let the ganache thicken slightly, then pour on top of the cheesecake. Refrigerate while you make the decorations.

8. To decorate: In a microwave-safe bowl, melt the chocolate chips in the microwave at 30-second intervals, stirring in between. Add to a pastry bag and pipe the chocolate onto acetate paper on top of your Gothic arch templates. Let them set completely before carefully peeling off.

9. Arrange the chocolate arches around the cheesecake and fill the middle with the fruits, flowers, and mint leaves, adding a couple of chocolate skulls, too.

| NOTE | Using a 6-inch (15-cm) springform pan for this recipe gives the cheesecake extra height, making it even more grand and impressive for all your gothic celebrations. But your Gothic arches can be any height you like! |

| TIP | Another way of getting your chocolate Gothic arches around the perimeter of your cheesecake is to leave them on the acetate paper until hardened, then wrap the acetate around the cheesecake, gently pressing the arches into the side so they stick, and then carefully pulling the paper away. |

Scary Berry Lemon Tarts

YIELD: 8 (4-inch, 10-cm) tarts ⚲ PREP TIME: 20 minutes, plus 1 hour and 15 minutes chill time ⚲ BAKE TIME: 22 minutes

PASTRY DOUGH

1 ¼ cups (155 g) all-purpose flour
¼ teaspoon sea salt
½ teaspoon powdered sugar
½ cup (115 g) cold unsalted butter, cut into cubes
2 to 3 tablespoons ice-cold water

LEMON FILLING

1 teaspoon unflavored gelatin powder
2 tablespoons cold water
¾ cup (180 ml) heavy cream, divided
1 cup (250 g) lemon curd

DECORATION

White modelling chocolate or fondant
Green modelling chocolate or fondant
Pink modelling chocolate or fondant
Red luster powder
8 medium strawberries
Royal icing
1 ¼ cups (300 ml) heavy cream

If you have been a fan of *The Great British Baking Show* since the beginning, you'll remember original judge, Mary Berry. After my appearance on the show back in 2019, my dear friend and illustrator Andrea Kett nicknamed me Scary Berry (in honor of how Mary can certainly be terrifying when she's judging a bake). Of course I had to create a recipe for this hilarious moniker! These Scary Berry tarts are delicious with a filling that comes together in minutes. Easy, quick, scrumptious . . . so maybe not so scary at all!

1. To make the dough: In a food processor, combine the flour, salt, and powdered sugar and pulse a couple of times to mix fully.

2. Add the cubed butter and pulse until the mixture resembles breadcrumbs (alternatively, you could do this with your hands).

3. Add the cold water, 1 tablespoon at a time, and pulse until the mixture forms large clumps and holds together when you press it in your hand.

4. Turn out onto a clean, dry surface and knead the dough a couple of times to bring it together. Form a ball, flatten, cover in plastic wrap, and refrigerate for 10 to 15 minutes.

(continued on next page)

(continued from previous page)

5. To make the filling: In a microwave-safe bowl, dissolve the gelatin powder in the cold water and let it bloom for 5 minutes. Then melt it in the microwave for 20 seconds or so, until it's liquid. Be careful as it can explode in the heat.

6. Mix 1 tablespoon of heavy cream into the gelatin. To the bowl of a stand mixer, add the remaining 11 tablespoons of cream and whip until soft peaks form. Add the gelatin mixture and mix fully.

7. Add the lemon curd and fold with a spatula until fully combined. Do not overmix. Cover and set aside.

8. Preheat the oven to 350°F (175°C). Remove the dough from the refrigerator and take off the plastic wrap. On a lightly floured surface, roll to a $1/8$-inch (3-mm) thickness. Roll the pastry onto your 8 pastry rings or mini tart molds, prick the base with a fork, then line the pastry with parchment paper.

9. Fill the parchment paper with weights. dry beans, or rice and blind bake for 12 minutes. Remove the weights and continue baking for another 10 minutes.

10. Remove from the oven and let cool completely.

11. Once cooled, fill the pastry cases with the lemon filling and set in the refrigerator for at least 1 hour.

12. To decorate: Roll a medium piece of white fondant into a sausage shape. Do the same with a smaller piece of green fondant. Roll them together then bend in half and roll again. Do these a few times until you get a marble effect.

13. Take a small piece of the marbled fondant and roll into a tentacle shape. Curve it and place on a piece of parchment paper to dry. Repeat this process several times, depending on how many tentacles you want. Some can stay straight, and some can be curved.

14. For the fondant tongues, roll a small piece of pink fondant into a thin sausage shape. Flatten and shape into a rolling tongue, then prick little holes all around it with a toothpick. Brush the sides with luster powder to give depth to the tongue.

15. Carve a mouth out of each strawberry, place the tongue in the middle, and pipe some teeth using the royal icing.

16. To the bowl of a stand mixer, add the heavy cream and whip until stiff peaks form. Add the whipped cream to a pastry bag fitted with a star nozzle.

17. Take the lemon tarts out of the refrigerator. One tart at a time, pipe a little dollop of cream in the middle, top with a strawberry, and arrange the tentacles around the edges.

18. Repeat process with the remaining tarts and serve.

Pumpkin Spice I-Scream

YIELD: : 16 i-screams ⚱ PREP TIME: 1 hour and 15 minutes ⚱ CHILL TIME: 2 hours

PUMPKIN ICE CREAM

1 large egg
2 large egg yolks
¾ cup (150 g) superfine sugar
1 ½ cups (360 ml) whole milk
1 ½ cups (360 ml) heavy
   whipping cream
1 cup (225 g) pumpkin purée
1 teaspoon ground cinnamon
1 teaspoon grated fresh nutmeg

WAFFLE CONES

16 waffle cones
Black luster dust

This recipe is an easy way to make everyone scream . . . for ice cream, that is. Using 2.16-inch by 1.77-inch (or 5.5-cm by 4.5-cm) pumpkin-shaped molds will make quick work of the ice cream part, but you have two options for the cones—decorate store-bought cones, or handmake them with a little added cocoa powder and black food coloring to make them lovely and dark. For the sake of speed and ease we'll go with the less-complicated version here, but know that the choice is yours!

1. To make the ice cream: In a large mixing bowl, whisk the egg and egg yolks until light and fluffy. Add the sugar and continue mixing until fully incorporated.

2. In a separate bowl, mix the milk and cream, then add to the egg mixture. Whisk until fully combined.

3. In a separate bowl, mix the pumpkin, cinnamon, and nutmeg. Add about 1 cup of the cream mixture and mix to combine, then pour it all back into the original milk and cream bowl and combine fully.

4. Pour into your ice cream maker and follow the manufacturer's instructions.

5. Once the ice cream is churned, pop it into a large pastry bag and pipe into the molds. Chill in the freezer for at least 2 hours, along with any leftover ice cream; this will be used later.

6. Meanwhile, decorate the cones. Dust the cones with the black luster powder using a pastry brush with bristles.

7. Fill the cones with the leftover ice cream, then pop the pumpkin-shaped ice cream tops out of the molds and place on top of each cone.

Bone Appe-Tiramisu

YIELD: Serves 8 ⚱ PREP TIME: 25 minutes ⚱ CHILL TIME: 5 hours or overnight

TIRAMISU

4 large eggs, separated
6 tablespoons granulated sugar, divided
2 cups (365 g) mascarpone cheese
1 tablespoon dark rum
1 cup (240 ml) strong,
    freshly brewed espresso
¼ cup (60 ml) coffee liqueur
24 to 26 lady fingers

DECORATION

Skeleton template
    (see QR code and scan)
3 tablespoons cocoa powder

My "bone daddy," my father, absolutely loves this dessert. I've turned a classic tiramisu recipe dark and dreamy with a lovely skeleton decoration on top. So simple yet so effective!

1. To make the tiramisu: In a medium bowl, combine the egg yolks and 3 tablespoons of the sugar and whisk until light and fluffy. Add the mascarpone and rum and continue mixing until fully combined. Set aside.

2. In the bowl of a stand mixer, whip the egg whites until stiff peaks form. Once frothy, add the remaining sugar, one tablespoon at a time.

3. Add one-third of the egg white mixture to the mascarpone mixture and fold gently to keep the air in. Repeat in thirds until all combined.

4. In a shallow bowl, combine the espresso with the liqueur. Lightly soak the lady fingers in the mixture on both sides and arrange half of them on the base of an 8 by 10-inch (20 by 25-cm) oval dish in one layer. You may need to break some to make them fit.

5. Spread out half the mascarpone mixture on top of the lady fingers and smooth over. Then repeat with another layer of soaked lady fingers and the rest of mascarpone. Smooth the top well and refrigerate for 1 hour.

6. To decorate: Remove from the refrigerator and top with your skeleton template. Dust with the cocoa powder, remove the stencil, and refrigerate for 4 hours or overnight.

Blue Moon Panna Cotta

YIELD: : Serves 8 ♀ PREP TIME: 10 minutes ♀ CHILL TIME: 2 hours

PANNA COTTA

5 sheets gelatin
1 ⅓ cups (300 ml) whole milk
3 ½ cups (800 ml) heavy cream
¾ cup (120 g) superfine sugar
2 vanilla bean pods, split
    lengthwise and scraped

BLUEBERRY REDUCTION

1 cup (150 g) blueberries
2 tablespoons granulated sugar
Splash of vanilla extract

DECORATION

Celestial sprinkles

I've developed this recipe with the winter solstice in mind. I've started a little tradition these last few years hosting a solstice dinner party with a séance after dessert. This celestial treat was last year's magical offering, and it became an instant favorite. You'll need full moon face silicone molds (1.69-inch or 4.3 cm diameter each) and your favorite ramekins for this recipe.

1. To make the panna cotta: Soak the gelatin sheets in a bowl of cold water for 5 minutes.
2. In a large saucepan, add the milk and cream over medium heat. Add the superfine sugar and vanilla bean seeds and stir to combine. Bring to a simmer then immediately remove from the heat.
3. Squeeze all the water from the gelatin sheets with your hands and add the gelatin to the hot milk. Stir until it has fully dissolved.
4. Pour into 8 individual ramekins leaving enough mixture to fill your crescent moon silicone molds, too.
5. Refrigerate the ramekins and the molds for at least 2 hours.
6. Meanwhile, make the blueberry reduction. In a small saucepan, combine the blueberries and sugar. Cook over medium heat until the fruit starts to break apart, then simmer for a couple of minutes.
7. Add the vanilla and stir. Pour through a sieve to strain; we are looking to retain just the liquid.
8. Take your ramekins out of the refrigerator and add a panna cotta moon to each one. Pour a little blueberry reduction on each one and top with the celestial sprinkles.

Banana Slug Pudding

VANILLA WAFERS

1/2 cup (115 g) salted butter, softened
2/3 cup (130 g) superfine sugar
1 large egg
4 teaspoons vanilla extract
1 1/2 cups (190 g) all-purpose flour
1/2 teaspoon baking powder
Pinch sea salt
Yellow food coloring
Brown food coloring

VANILLA CUSTARD

1 cup (240 ml) cold whole milk
2 1/2 ounces (70 g) vanilla pudding mix
1/2 (14-ounce, or 397-g) can
    sweetened condensed milk
1 teaspoon vanilla extract
6 ounces (170 g) whipped topping,
    such as Cool Whip, thawed
5 to 6 bananas, peeled and sliced

In many southern American states, this dessert consisting of layers of vanilla custard, sliced banana, and vanilla wafer cookies topped with whipped cream is served at Sunday dinners and/or family reunions. I thought it would be fun to turn this very traditional recipe on its head with a couple of gross slugs . . . made from wafer cookies, of course. We'll make them from scratch using a low-effort yet scrumptious recipe.

1. Preheat the oven to 350°F (175°C) and line two baking sheets with parchment paper or a silicone mat.

2. To make the wafers: In the bowl of an electric mixer fitted with the paddle attachment, beat the butter and sugar until light and fluffy on medium-high speed.

3. Add the egg and vanilla and continue mixing.

4. Turn the speed to low and add the flour, baking powder, and salt. Add a few drops yellow coloring and continue mixing. If the batter looks too dry, add a little milk.

5. Reserve one-quarter of the dough to shape like slugs. Scoop the rest into 2-teaspoon size dollops and place on one of the prepared baking sheets.

6. Shape the reserved dough into banana slug shapes. Research what these looks like beforehand. Add to the second prepared baking sheet.

7. Bake the dollops for 12 to 14 minutes and the slugs for about 8 minutes, before they start browning.

8. Remove and let cool completely, then paint patches on the slugs with the brown food coloring.

9. To make the custard: In a medium bowl, mix the milk with the vanilla pudding mix for a few minutes. Then add the condensed milk and continue mixing.

10. Add the vanilla then carefully fold in the Cool Whip.

11. Layer the dessert (see Note) starting with the wafer cookies, then the banana slices, and custard mixture. Repeat, making sure you finish with the custard layer. Top with a couple of banana slug wafers and serve.

NOTE | I've used individual vintage-style milkshake glasses for my serving vessels, but you can use one big dish or anything else you like. The display is up to you!

Wraith's Winter Pudding Cake Pops

YIELD: : 36 to 40 pops ⚱ PREP TIME: 2 hours, plus 1 hour chill time ⚱ BAKE TIME: 30 to 35 minutes

GINGER CAKE

1 ¼ cups (155 g) all-purpose flour
½ teaspoon baking powder
½ teaspoon baking soda
¼ teaspoon sea salt
2 tablespoons ground ginger
½ tablespoon ground cinnamon
¼ teaspoon grated fresh nutmeg
½ cup plus 1 tablespoon (125 g)
   unsalted butter
⅔ cup (165 g) packed light brown sugar
3 tablespoons molasses
⅔ cup (165 ml) whole milk
1 extra-large egg
½ cup (50 g) pecans, roughly chopped
2 tablespoons salted caramel sauce

CHOCOLATE COATING

24 ounces (680 g) dark or
   milk chocolate, chopped

DECORATION

40 lollipop sticks
Round edible pearls for the eyes
Black edible ink pen
1 cup (165 g) white chocolate chips
Holly leaf and red berry sprinkles

These little evil cake pops are inspired by Christmas puddings, also known as plum pudding or figgy pudding in the US. Originating in medieval England, Christmas pudding is a sweet dried-fruit cake that gets soaked in alcohol, is lit ablaze, and then presented at the table on Christmas Day. If you're like me and are not a fan of the Christmas pudding flavors but love the traditions around it, you're in luck because I'm using my favorite ginger cake recipe for these pops for a more widely beloved, delicious Christmas flavor.

1. Preheat the oven to 320°F (160°C) and grease a 9-inch (23-cm) pan with butter and flour or nonstick spray. Set aside.

2. To make the cake: Into a bowl, sift the flour, baking powder, baking soda, salt, ginger, cinnamon, and nutmeg and set aside.

3. In a large pan, melt the butter, brown sugar, and molasses over medium-low heat, stirring constantly until combined. Slowly add the milk and warm through. Remove from the heat and mix in the dry ingredients until fully combined. Add the egg and the pecans and mix.

4. Pour the batter into your prepared pan and bake for 30 to 35 minutes, or until a skewer inserted in the center comes out clean.

(continued on next page)

(continued from previous page)

5. While the cake is still slightly warm, crumble it into the bowl of a stand mixer, add the caramel sauce, and mix well. The steam of the warm cake should help the mixture come together, but you can add more sauce if needed.

6. Scoop out large tablespoons of the cake mixture and roll into balls. Place them on a baking sheet lined with parchment paper and freeze for 1 hour.

7. Remove from the refrigerator and make a couple of small round dents in each ball; this is where the eyes will be placed. Return to the refrigerator.

8. To prepare the coating: In a heat-safe measuring cup, add the dark or milk chocolate and microwave at 30-second intervals, stirring each time.

9. Working with 2 or 3 balls at a time, keeping the rest refrigerated, dip the end of a lollipop stick about $\frac{1}{2}$ inch into the chocolate, then insert into the center of the cake ball, pushing it halfway through. Dip the cake ball into the chocolate until fully covered and shake off the excess.

10. Place the clean end of the stick into a Styrofoam block to set upright, and continue dipping the rest of the cake balls.

11. To decorate: Once all are dipped and the chocolate fully set (about 20 minutes), use a little melted chocolate to glue the edible pearls into the eye sockets created earlier. Draw the iris with the black edible ink pen.

12. In a heat-safe measuring cup, add the white chocolate and microwave at 30-second intervals, stirring each time. Spoon some of the melted white chocolate on top of the pops and let it drip a little, avoiding the eyes.

13. Top with the holly and berry sprinkles.

TIP

To make angry-looking pudding pops, try piping some V-shaped eyebrows with extra melted chocolate and adding candy flames instead of white chocolate at the top. You can make the flames by melting red, orange, and yellow Jolly Ranchers on a silicone mat in the oven and creating swirls with a toothpick. A fitting nod to the flaming Christmas puddings of old!

Crispy Rice Trick-or-Treats

YIELD: 12 crispy rice treats ☙ PREP TIME: 25 minutes

10 ounces (285 g) white candy melts

4 thick pretzel rods

10 ounces (285 g) mini marshmallows, plus 4 for the chicken bone version

5 ounces (140 g) golden or white marzipan

4 thin pretzel sticks

½ cup (115 g) salted butter

½ teaspoon vanilla extract

⅔ cup (165 g) smooth peanut butter

8 cups (320 g) crispy rice cereal

These crispy rice treats are not only delicious but so much fun to make! Some are meant to look like chicken drumsticks, but others have a human leg instead of a "chicken bone" making them look like someone had quite the trick pulled on them this spooky season.

1. In a heat-safe bowl, add the candy melts and microwave at 30-second intervals, stirring well in between.

2. To make the chicken bone version: Cut the 4 thick pretzel rods in half width wise with a sharp knife. Set aside.

3. Using scissors, cut the 4 mini marshmallows in half lengthways and attach them to each of the uncut side of the pretzel rods with a little of the melted candy melts. Place them on a silicone mat or parchment paper and leave them to set.

4. Once the marshmallows are secured in place, dip the entire pretzel rod into the candy melts starting from the marshmallow end up to just before where your fingers are holding it. It should now look like a bone. Place them back on the silicone mat.

5. If you feel they need to be dipped twice for a better shape, go ahead and dip them again after they have fully set.

(continued on next page)

(continued from previous page)

6. To make the human leg version: Wrap bits of marzipan around the thin pretzel sticks and using a picture of a leg as reference (I used a Barbie leg for mine), mold the marzipan to make it look like a human leg.

7. In a medium-large pan, melt the butter over low heat. Add the marshmallows and vanilla. When they're almost fully melted, add the peanut butter. Stir until fully melted. Add the crispy rice cereal and mix well. Remove from the heat.

8. Wrap about $1/3$ cup of the crispy rice mixture around each chicken bone and human leg pretzel, shaping them like a chicken drumstick with your hands. Work quickly before the mixture sets.

9. Place on a serving tray and choose your treat . . . or trick.

TIP | Drizzle the drumsticks with caramel sauce for an even more realistic look.

Macabre
Cakes
and
Bakes

Cauldron Cakes

YIELD: 12 mini cauldrons ❦ PREP TIME: 15 minutes ❦ BAKE TIME: 20 to 25 minutes

BANANA CAKE BATTER

2 cups (260 g) cake flour
1 teaspoon baking powder
1 teaspoon baking soda
3/4 teaspoon sea salt
1/2 cup (115 g) unsalted butter, softened
1 1/3 cups (256 g) granulated sugar
2 large eggs
1 teaspoon vanilla extract
1 cup (240 ml) buttermilk
3 medium ripe bananas, mashed
1/2 cup (50 g) walnuts, roughly chopped

VANILLA BUTTERCREAM

1 cup (225 g) salted butter, softened
3 1/4 cups (400 g) powdered sugar,
    sifted
1/2 teaspoon vanilla extract
1 to 2 tablespoons whole milk (optional)
Red food coloring
Yellow food coloring

These cauldron cakes are inspired by the ones in the wizarding world of Harry Potter. Instead of chocolate cake I've used an amazing vintage recipe for banana bread. The moist sponge is stuffed into the plastic cauldrons (they're from eBay!) and topped with flames made of vanilla buttercream. We don't need to go to Honeydukes, we can make our own!

1. Preheat the oven to 350°F (175° C) and grease a 9 by 13-inch (23 by 33-cm) baking pan.

2. To make the cake batter: In a large bowl, sift together the flour, baking powder, baking soda, and salt. Set aside.

3. In the bowl of an electric mixer fitted with the paddle attachment, combine the butter and sugar and beat at medium-high speed until light and fluffy. Add the eggs, one at a time, and then the vanilla, and continue mixing.

4. Add half the flour mixture and continue mixing. Then half the buttermilk, the other half of the flour, and finish with the remaining buttermilk.

5. Add the mashed bananas and walnuts and continue mixing until all is incorporated.

(continued on next page)

(continued from previous page)

6. Transfer the batter to the prepared pan and bake for 20 to 25 minutes, or until a toothpick inserted in the center comes out clean. Leave to cool.

7. To make the buttercream: In the bowl of an electric mixer fitted with the paddle attachment, add the butter and beat at high speed until creamy. Lower the speed and add the powdered sugar, 1 tablespoon at a time. Add the vanilla and continue mixing.

8. You want a spreadable consistency so if the buttercream is too dry, add a little milk. If too wet, add more sugar.

9. Divide the buttercream into two bowls. Add red food coloring to one and yellow food coloring to the other.

10. Add the red buttercream to one side of a large pastry bag and the yellow buttercream to the other side. Flatten the bag a bit to let them mix slightly in the middle. Set aside.

11. Break the banana cake into pieces and fill the plastic cauldrons to just below the top.

12. Cut the bottom of the pastry bag straight, around $1/3$ inch (1 cm), and then cut an inverted V. Push the buttercream to the end and push out the filling until both the yellow and red buttercreams come out together looking like flames.

13. Pipe your cauldrons and serve.

Black Cat Mini Swiss Rolls

YIELD: 6 to 8 black cat rolls ❧ PREP TIME: 45 minutes, plus 30 minutes chill time ❧ BAKE TIME: 10 to 12 minutes

CHOCOLATE SPONGE

6 medium eggs
1 cup (195 g) superfine sugar
1/2 cup minus 1 tablespoon (45 g)
    cocoa powder
Black food coloring

VANILLA CREAM FILLING

1 cup (240 ml) heavy cream
2 tablespoons powdered sugar
1 teaspoon vanilla extract
1/2 cup (170 g) semi-sweet
    chocolate chips, melted

If you have ever made a Swiss roll or cake roll before, then these little felines will be the purr-fect variation for you to tackle. We are making two separate Swiss-style sponges—one for the rolls and one for the cat faces and tails. Use two 9 by 13-inch (23 by 33-cm) baking pans that are about 1/3 inch (1 cm) high; they're specific to Swiss roll baking.

1. Preheat the oven to 350°F (175°C) and line two 9 by 13-inch (23 by 33-cm) Swiss roll pans with parchment paper.

2. To make the sponge: In the bowl of an electric mixer fitted with the whisk attachment, combine the eggs and sugar and mix on high speed for 6 to 8 minutes, or until the mixture is pale and fluffy. This is called the ribbon stage as you should be able to pull a ribbon of mixture with the whisk after mixing.

3. Sift in the cocoa powder and add the food coloring. Fold with a spatula, making sure not to knock out too much air.

4. Divide the mixture equally between the two pans. Spread to the corners and level the batter with an offset spatula.

5. Bake for 10 to 12 minutes until the sponge springs back to the touch.

(continued on next page)

(continued from previous page)

6. Lay out a damp dish towel on your work surface and place a piece of parchment paper larger than the sponge on top. Using oven gloves, remove the first sponge from the oven and immediately turn out onto the prepared paper. Set the other sponge aside.

7. Use the paper and dish towel to help you tightly roll the sponge up from each of the longer edges so that the meet in the middle. Set aside.

8. To make the cream filling: In a large bowl, whisk the cream with the sugar and vanilla until soft peaks form and it thickens to a spreadable consistency.

9. Unroll the first sponge and place onto a piece of plastic wrap. Spread a thin layer of cream filling all the way to the edge. Reroll the cake to the middle from both sides tightly.

10. Slice the roll down the middle where the two rolls meet so you have two long cake rolls. Place each roll seam side down onto plastic wrap. Wrap each cake roll tightly with the plastic wrap, pulling the ends tightly to keep everything in place.

11. Refrigerate the cake rolls for 30 minutes.

12. Meanwhile, cut out the cat faces and tails from the second sponge. You can use a cookie cutter for this or simply draw a cat face shape (including the ears!) and tail out of paper and cut around it. Each face should be approximately 2 inches (5 ½ cm) in diameter.

13. Remove the rolls from the refrigerator and unwrap. Slice each with a sharp knife into 6 to 8 mini rolls depending how big you want them.

14. Spread a little melted chocolate onto one side of the cat faces and tails and stick to the front and back of each mini roll. Let them set completely before serving.

NOTE | If your rolls end up on the larger side, make sure to increase the size of your cat faces and tails to be proportional.

TIP | If you find that your chocolate sponge is cracking while rolling, add ½ cup (65 g) all-purpose flour and 1 tablespoon of vegetable oil to stabilize.

The Worst "Pie" in London

YIELD: 6 "pies" • PREP TIME: 10 minutes • BAKE TIME: 30 to 35 minutes

½ cup (115 g) stick margarine
¼ cup (60 ml) vegetable oil
1 ¼ cups (245 g) superfine sugar
3 small eggs
1 ½ cups (190 g) all-purpose flour
1 teaspoon baking powder
1 teaspoon sea salt
½ cup (120 ml) buttermilk
2 teaspoons vanilla extract
1 teaspoon almond extract
1 (3.88-ounce, or 110-g) jar orange curd
1 (17 ounces, or 500 g) packet
    golden marzipan
Cocoa powder for brushing
Red gel food coloring

Inspired by Mrs. Lovett's pies in the musical *Sweeney Todd*, this "pie" isn't a pie at all. It is an almond sponge stacked between layers of orange curd and covered in golden marzipan but shaped like a traditional British pie. The fingers and ear are also made of marzipan. Don't be afraid to do a little sculpting! Body parts are the first things I ever sculpted in food and looking at real pictures helps to get the right result.

1. Preheat the oven to 350°F (175°C) and spray two 9 by 13-inch (23 by 33-cm) baking pans with nonstick spray, or use butter, and flour them.

2. In the bowl of an electric mixer fitted with the paddle attachment, cream together the margarine, oil, and sugar until light and fluffy. Add the eggs, one at a time, and continue mixing.

3. In a separate bowl, sift together the flour, baking powder, and salt. In another bowl, mix the buttermilk and vanilla and almond extracts. Add the flour and buttermilk mixtures to the margarine mixture on low speed, alternating in thirds, and mix until well combined.

(continued on next page)

(continued from previous page)

4. Divide the batter between the two pans and bake in the middle of the oven for 30 to 35 minutes, or until a toothpick inserted in the middle comes out clean.

5. Let the cakes cool completely on a wire rack.

6. Level the cakes and cut out 6 cake circles from each tray with a 4-inch (9.5-cm) round cookie cutter. Add the orange curd to the top of one circle and cover with another cake circle. Brush some extra curd on the entire outside of the cake stack to help the marzipan stick. Repeat with the remaining cakes and curd.

7. Cover each cake in marzipan and pinch the top edge with your index finger and thumb to crimp to look like a pie crust. Brush the edges with cocoa powder to make them look browned.

8. Sculpt some of the leftover marzipan into fingers and ears. This is easier to do than you think, and it helps to look at your own fingers and someone else's ear as reference.

9. Add red food coloring to some orange curd. Cut a cross in the middle of each pie and fill the center with the red-colored curd. Insert some of the fingers. Repeat with the remaining pies.

10. Serve on a tray with some scattered ears and leftover fingers.

TIPS

You can use orange marmalade in place of curd if you wish.

If you're lucky to have an airbrush kit, that will make quick work of the cocoa powder dusting.

Feel free to chop any leftover fingers into smaller bits and add some red food coloring to enhance your presentation.

Chocolate Monster Cake

YIELD: Serves 8 ❧ PREP TIME: 50 minutes, plus 20 minutes chill time ❧ BAKE TIME: 35 to 40 minutes

CHOCOLATE CAKE

1 3/4 cups (220 g) all-purpose flour
2 cups (390 g) superfine sugar
3/4 cup (70 g) cocoa powder
2 teaspoons baking soda
1 teaspoon baking powder
1 teaspoon kosher salt
1 cup (240 ml) buttermilk
1/2 cup (120 ml) vegetable oil
2 extra-large eggs,
    at room temperature
1 teaspoon vanilla extract
1 cup (240 ml) freshly
    brewed coffee

CHOCOLATE FROSTING

8 ounces (225 g) dark chocolate
    (60–70 percent cocoa solids),
    chopped
3/4 cup (180 ml) heavy cream
2 tablespoons golden syrup
    or corn syrup
1 1/2 tablespoons cocoa powder,
    sifted
1 teaspoon instant coffee
1/2 teaspoon vanilla extract
1/3 cup (75 ml) sour cream
Black gel food coloring

FONDANT TEETH

2 ounces (55 g) white fondant
2 ounces (55 g) yellow fondant
2 ounces (55 g) orange fondant

GOOEY BLOOD

Honey
Red food coloring

Originally created for my school of witchery, this delicious and moist chocolate cake gets scary with an open mouth and candy corn teeth. I tried to make the candy corn from scratch but take my word for it, it's not worth it! In place of buying actual candy corn, I made the teeth out of fondant in candy corn colors.

(continued on next page)

(continued from previous page)

1. Preheat the oven to 350°F (175°C) and spray two 6 by 3-inch (15 by 7-cm) cake pans with nonstick spray or brush with vegetable oil.

2. To make the cake: Into the bowl of an electric mixer fitted with the paddle attachment, sift the flour, sugar, cocoa powder, baking soda, baking powder, and salt and mix on low speed until combined.

3. Add the buttermilk, oil, eggs, and vanilla and continue mixing until fully incorporated.

4. Add the coffee and mix until just combined. The batter will be thin.

5. Divide the batter between the pans and bake in the oven for 35 to 40 minutes, or until a toothpick inserted in the center of the cake comes out clean. Let the cakes cool completely on a wire rack.

6. Meanwhile, make the frosting. In a medium heat-proof bowl, add the chocolate and set aside.

7. In a small saucepan, combine the cream and syrup and bring it to just before the boiling point over medium heat. Pour over the chopped chocolate and let it stand for a couple of minutes. Stir until fully incorporated.

8. Add the cocoa powder, coffee, vanilla, sour cream, and food coloring, and mix well. Cover and refrigerate for about 20 minutes, or until thickened enough to be a pipeable consistency.

9. Place your first cake onto a cake board or plate, spread a layer of frosting, and top with the other cake layer. Cut out a half-moon-shaped, 1-inch-long chunk from the left and right sides of the top cake and place above the cuts to make the open mouth shape. Cover the mouth and rest of cake in frosting. Smooth with a spatula. Refrigerate while making the teeth.

10. To make the candy corn teeth: Roll the three colored fondants into long tubes. Place the yellow at the bottom, orange in the middle, and white on top (it helps to brush a little water in between so they stick together). Flatten them with a rolling pin into a long ribbon, then cut out triangles using a zig-zag motion.

11. Shape each triangle into a pointy tooth and insert a small toothpick into the flat bottom. Place on a piece of parchment and let them harden for about an hour

12. Add the teeth to the top and bottom of the opened cake mouth, then fill a pastry bag with the leftover frosting and pipe scrolls and shells patterns to decorate the cake in grand Victorian style.

13. To make the honey blood: In a small bowl, mix a bit of honey with red food coloring. Drip some edible blood onto the teeth in the cake to finish it off.

NOTE

Research online scroll and shell pattern piping techniques for the proper form and to get inspired for how to decorate this cake. The tips for your pastry bag that you will need to get the look are star piping tips—a #32 for shells and the smaller the better for scrolls.

Cemetery Traybake

YIELD: Serves 18 to 20 ♀ PREP TIME: 20 minutes BAKE TIME: 50 to 55 minutes

CHOCOLATE CAKE

1¾ cups (220 g) all-purpose flour
2 cups (390 g) superfine sugar
¾ cup (70 g) cocoa powder
2 teaspoons baking soda
1 teaspoon baking powder
1 teaspoon kosher salt
1 cup (240 ml) buttermilk
½ cup (120 ml) vegetable oil
2 extra-large eggs, at room
temperature
1 teaspoon vanilla extract
1 cup (240 ml) freshly
brewed coffee

CHOCOLATE BUTTERCREAM

1 cup (225 g) unsalted butter,
at room temperature
3 ½ cups (440 g) powdered
sugar
½ cup (50 g) cocoa powder
3 tablespoons heavy cream
1 teaspoon vanilla extract
Pinch kosher salt
½ teaspoon instant coffee
1 tablespoon hot water

ZUCCHINI SPONGE

1 cup (225 g) chopped zucchini,
cooked, puréed, and drained
½ cup (120 ml) vegetable oil
1 cup (200 g) granulated sugar
½ cup (120 ml) milk, any type
2 large eggs
1 cup (125 g) all-purpose flour
1 ½ teaspoons ground cinnamon
1 teaspoon baking soda
¼ teaspoon baking powder
½ teaspoon kosher salt
1 teaspoon vanilla extract

DECORATION

White gel food coloring
Edible flowers such as daisies or
white clover

I originally styled this cake as a spring traybake, with white skeletons adorned with daisies and white clover; however, it really lends itself to be a vibrant and colorful Day of the Dead celebration cake too! The base is chocolate cake, and we top it with a moist zucchini sponge "moss" for two cakes in one. To really get that patch of grass and dirt look, use a 9 by 13-inch (23 by 33-cm) baking pan; for our dancing friends, Nordic Ware makes a great Spooky Skeleton Cakelet pan.

(continued on next page)

(continued from previous page)

1. Preheat the oven to 350°F (175°C) and grease with oil or butter a 9 by 13-inch (23 by 33-cm) baking pan and your skeleton pan.

2. To make the chocolate cake: Into the bowl of an electric mixer fitted with the paddle attachment, sift the flour, sugar, cocoa powder, baking soda, baking powder, and salt and mix on low speed until combined.

3. Add the buttermilk, oil, eggs, and vanilla and continue mixing until fully incorporated. Mix in the coffee.

4. Pour the batter into the skeleton cake tin three-quarters of the way up. Then add the rest to the baking pan.

5. Bake for 30 to 35 minutes, checking the skeletons after 20 minutes or so as they will bake faster. Leave the cakes to cool in the pans.

6. To make the buttercream: In the bowl of an electric mixer fitted with the paddle attachment, beat the butter 2 to 3 minutes, until light and fluffy. Then turn the speed down to low and gradually add the sugar. Add the cocoa powder, cream, vanilla, and salt and mix until all is well combined. In a small bowl, dissolve the instant coffee in the hot water and add to the mixture.

7. Level the cakes while still in the pan keeping the leftovers aside in a bowl as we will use this as part of the cemetery "moss."

8. Spread a layer of chocolate frosting on the main cake and place the skeletons on top. Set aside.

9. To make the zucchini sponge: In the bowl of an electric mixer fitted with a paddle attachment combine the zucchini, oil, sugar, milk, eggs, flour, cinnamon, baking soda, baking powder, salt, and vanilla and mix until fully combined. Pour the batter into 24 muffin cups filling them up three-quarters of the way. In your oven set to 350°F (175°C), bake for 20 to 25 minutes or until an inserted toothpick comes out clean. Let them cool fully.

10. While the muffins are cooling, brush some white gel food coloring onto the skeletons to define the bones.

11. Crumble half of the zucchini muffins into the bowl with the chocolate cake scraps and mix them well to create the final "moss." Add more muffin crumbles if you'd like the color a bit more moss green and less dirt brown. Still not mossy enough? Mix in a little moss-green food coloring.

12. Decorate with the zucchini-chocolate moss and edible flowers. Serve at your next festive cemetery gathering.

TIPS

Want to make more of a graveyard scene? Add small plastic headstones among the dancing skeletons. Or, if you're feeling adventurous, sculpt out of fondant.

To flip the theme of this traybake to Dia de Los Muertos, change the colors of your edible flowers to oranges, purples, reds, blues, and yellows, and sprinkle on some edible glitter.

Poison Apple Cakes

YIELD: 8 apples ⚬ PREP TIME: 10 minutes ⚬ BAKE TIME: 20 to 25 minutes

CINNAMON SPONGE

1 cup (240 ml) vegetable oil
2 cups (400 g) granulated sugar
4 large eggs
2 cups (250 g) all-purpose flour
1 teaspoon baking powder
¼ teaspoon sea salt
3 tablespoons ground cinnamon

APPLE FILLING

1 tablespoon unsalted butter
2 Granny Smith apples, cored, peeled,
    and chopped into small chunks
Pinch sea salt
Pinch ground cloves
Pinch ground nutmeg
1 ½ tablespoons maple syrup

BROWN SUGAR FROSTING

½ cup (115 g) salted butter
1 cup (220 g) packed dark brown sugar
¼ cup (60 ml) whole milk
Powdered sugar, sifted

DECORATION

White fondant
Water-based food coloring in red, green,
    yellow, and brown
Apple stems and leaves

Trick (but actually treat) your guests by placing some of these in a bowl full of mixed fruit. What's amazing about this bake is that the cake and frosting recipes are vintage; I've had them on a handwritten piece of paper since I was a teenager! I've added an apple filling because you know what they say—an apple a day . . .

1. Preheat the oven to 350°F (175°C) and grease with vegetable oil or spray with non-stick spray two 8-count semi-sphere (2.55-inch, or 6-cm each) silicone molds.

2. To make the sponge: In an electric mixer fitted with the paddle attachment, mix the oil, sugar, and eggs on medium speed. Add the flour, baking powder, salt, and cinnamon and continue mixing until fully incorporated.

5. Divide the batter equally between the semi spheres and bake for 20 to 25 minutes, or until a toothpick comes out clean.

4. Meanwhile, make the filling. In a large pan melt the butter over medium heat. Add the chopped apple with a pinch of salt. Cook for 3 minutes, or until the apples start to brown. Add the cloves, nutmeg, and maple syrup and continue cooking until the sauce thickens a little. Set aside.

(continued on next page)

(continued from previous page)

5. To make the frosting: In a saucepan, combine the butter and brown sugar and bring to a simmer over medium- low heat. Add the milk and bring it to a boil.

6. Remove from heat and let cool slightly. Add enough powdered sugar to give it the right consistency to frost the cakes; we are looking for a spreadable consistency.

7. After your cakes are baked and cooled, level them with a serrated knife.

8. Using a melon baller, make a hole in the middle of one semi-sphere and fill with the apple filling.

9. Spread some frosting onto the flat bottom and attach another semi-sphere, flat sides together. Carve a little indentation on the top where the stem will go.

10. To decorate: Roll your fondant to a $1/8$-inch (3-mm) thickness and smooth over the cakes.

11. Brush some yellow food coloring at the top and base of the apple. Top it with some green food coloring and then with brush strokes of red food coloring, from the base to the top.

12. Dip the bristles of a brush in the brown food coloring and flick them towards the apple to create some dots. Brush a bit more brown around where the stem will go.

13. Attach a real apple stem and leaf to the apple cakes for a realistic look.

NOTES

You'll have enough cinnamon batter left over for two more apples (for a total of 10). You can save and bake another round in your semi-sphere molds or just make a few muffins on the side.

Use a real pink lady apple for reference when painting your cakes.

If you don't have any real apple stems or leaves leftover from your harvest, you can make them out of fondant.

TIPS

I'm pretty sure originally this cake was meant to be a traybake. For a less time-consuming outing, layer the sponge, filling, and frosting in a baking tray for apple cake slices. It will be just as delicious and perfect when you need to whip up something festive in a hurry!

This is another recipe where an airbrush tool would come in handy.

Creepmas Present Pistachio Cupcakes

YIELD: 12 cupcakes ❧ PREP TIME: 10 minutes ❧ BAKE TIME: 16 to 18 minutes

PISTACHIO CAKE

1 ½ cups (190 g) all-purpose flour
1 teaspoon baking powder
½ teaspoon baking soda
1 teaspoon sea salt
½ cup (115 g) unsalted butter,
    at room temperature
1 cup (195 g) superfine sugar
1 large egg
¾ cup (180 ml) buttermilk
3 tablespoons pistachio butter
    (see recipe on page 35)
1 teaspoon vanilla extract
1 tablespoon almond extract
Green food coloring

STRAWBERRY FROSTING

4 ounces (115 g) fresh
    strawberries, quartered
1 cup (500 g) salted butter,
    at room temperature
4 cups (500 g) powdered sugar
1 teaspoon vanilla extract
Pink food coloring

DECORATION

Large edible pearls
Black edible ink pen
Black luster dust
Red fondant

These little creepers are so adorable that you soon forget they're meant to be a little scary. From Creepmas to birthdays, these would suit any occasion in which presents are exchanged! I've gone with a pistachio cupcake and strawberry buttercream; the flavors and colors complement each other perfectly and call to mind the festively spooky winter season.

(continued on next page)

(continued from previous page)

1. Preheat the oven to 350°F (175°C) and line a 12-cup cupcake pan with paper liners.

2. To make the cake: Into a medium bowl, sift the flour, baking powder, baking soda, and salt and set aside.

3. In the bowl of an electric mixer fitted with the paddle attachment, beat the butter and sugar on medium-high speed until light and fluffy.

4. Add the egg and continue mixing, then add half the buttermilk and mix until combined.

5. Turn the mixer to low and add half the flour mixture, followed by the rest of the buttermilk, then the remaining flour mixture..

6. Add the pistachio butter and vanilla and almond extracts, followed by the green food coloring, and mix until fully combined.

7. Divide the batter equally among the cupcake liners and bake for 16 to 18 minutes or until a toothpick inserted in the middle comes out clean.

8. To make the frosting: In a small saucepan, cook the quartered strawberries with 1 tablespoon of water over medium heat until they start breaking up.

9. Mash them into a pulp with a potato masher and continue cooking in the pan, stirring constantly to remove some of the moisture. You are looking for a paste consistency. Leave to cool completely.

10. In the bowl of an electric mixer, beat the butter on high speed until light and fluffy. Lower the speed and slowly add the powdered sugar, continue mixing until fully incorporated then add the vanilla.

11. Scrape the sides and bottom of the bowl, then add the strawberry purée, mixing in with a spatula. Add the pink food coloring to enhance the deep pink shade.

12. Fill a large pastry bag, fitted with a grass piping tip, with the strawberry frosting and set aside.

13. To decorate: Paint a small iris onto the edible pearls and dust some black luster dust onto the sides to give the eyes a Tim Burton–style look.

14. Cut a well in the top of each cupcake and fill with a little frosting. Add the eyes and pipe the hair-like frosting around the eyes and on top of the cupcake.

15. Sculpt bows with the red fondant and place them on top of the cupcakes. How ornate or simple is up to how fancy you like to wrap your presents!

Vintage Witch Cakes

YIELD: 12 witches ⚶ **PREP TIME:** 10 minutes, plus 30 minutes chill time ⚶ **BAKE TIME:** 10 to 15 minutes

COCONUT CAKE

¼ cup (55 g) vegan butter
½ cup (100 g) superfine sugar
¼ cup (60 ml) plain vegan yogurt
¼ teaspoon coconut extract
¼ cup (30 ml) coconut milk
½ tablespoon white wine vinegar
1 cup minus 2 tablespoons (115 g)
    cake flour
½ teaspoon baking powder
¼ teaspoon baking soda
¼ teaspoon sea salt
¼ cup (25 g) sweetened
    desiccated coconut

COCONUT FROSTING

½ cup (115 g) vegan butter, softened
¼ cup (50 g) coconut cream
¼ teaspoon coconut extract
2 ½ cups (315 g) powdered sugar
Orange gel food coloring
Green gel food coloring

DECORATION

24 blue candies such as mini M&M's
12 paper witch hats with
    black pom-poms
    (see QR code and scan)

The idea for these cakes comes from the September/October 1973 issue of *Celebrate* magazine. It featured a large witch head cake that I loved, but I thought making the witch into individual cakes would be more fun. The cakes are finished with little hats that you can easily make with cardboard or construction paper and a pom-pom. I've gone for my best vegan coconut sponge which is just as good (if not better!) than any cake that uses eggs and dairy, so no one is missing out on any of the witchy deliciousness.

1. Preheat the oven to 325°F (165°C) and grease two 6-cavity semi-sphere silicone molds (with each cavity being 2 ½ inches, or 6 ½ cm in diameter) with vegetable oil or non-stick spray.

2. To make the cake: In the bowl of an electric mixer fitted with the paddle attachment, mix the butter and sugar on high speed until light and fluffy. Add the yogurt, coconut extract, coconut milk, and vinegar and continue mixing.

5. Into a large bowl, sift together the cake flour, baking powder, baking soda, and salt. Then slowly add to the wet ingredients.

1. Add the desiccated coconut and mix until it's fully incorporated.

(continued on next page)

(continued from previous page)

5. Pour into your molds and bake for 10 to 15 minutes, or until a toothpick inserted in the middle comes out clean. Leave to cool completely.

6. To make the frosting: Mix the butter and coconut cream in the bowl of an electric mixer until it all comes together on high speed. Add the coconut extract.

7. Reduce the speed to low and slowly add the powdered sugar.

8. Turn the speed to high and continue mixing 4 to 5 minutes, until the frosting is light and fluffy.

9. Remove about one-quarter of the frosting to a separate bowl and color it orange. Color the rest of the frosting with the green food coloring.

10. Once the cakes are cooled, frost in green using an offset spatula, smooth well. Using the remaining green frosting, pipe the noses with a petal pipping tip, pressing the bag from the base and piping into a straight line upwards. Refrigerate for 30 minutes.

11. Fill a pastry bag, fitted with a small round tip, with the rest of the green frosting, and another pastry bag with the orange frosting using a grass tip.

12. To decorate: Take the cakes out of the refrigerator and attach the blue candies for eyes with a little green frosting, then use the pastry bag to pipe the eye lids.

13. Pipe the hair with the orange frosting and finish them off with their little paper hats.

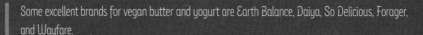
NOTE | Some excellent brands for vegan butter and yogurt are Earth Balance, Daiya, So Delicious, Forager, and Wayfare.

Scary Teddy Cake

VANILLA SPONGE

4 cups (500 g) all-purpose flour
3 ½ teaspoons baking powder
½ teaspoon sea salt
2 cups (450 g) unsalted butter, softened
2 ½ cups (500 g) granulated sugar
8 large eggs
¼ cup vanilla extract
1 ½ cups (360 ml) buttermilk

CHOCOLATE FROSTING

12 ounces (340 g) dark chocolate,
    60–70 percent cocoa solids
2 cups (450 g) salted butter,
    at room temperature
2 extra-large egg yolks
2 teaspoons vanilla extract
2 ½ cups (315 g) powdered sugar
2 tablespoons instant coffee
4 teaspoons hot water
Red gel food coloring
Pink gel food coloring

DECORATION

Brown fondant
White fondant
Skewers, toothpicks, and/or bubble tea
    straws for added support

To complement the scary teddy cookies (page 29) I have developed this rather disturbing teddy cake. Available for children's birthdays and christenings, the vanilla sponge makes a sturdy cake that's easy to carve while still maintaining a delicious flavor. To get our bear-y scary look, we'll need two 3 by 6-inch (7.5 by 15-cm) round cake pans for the body and two 2 by 6-inch (5 by 15-cm) semi-sphere cake pans for the head.

1. Preheat the oven to 325°F (165°C) and spray the 6-inch (15-cm) round cake pans and two 6-inch (15-cm) semi-sphere cake pans with non-stick spray or brush them with vegetable oil.

2. To make the sponge: Into a large bowl, sift the flour, baking powder, and salt. Set aside.

3. In the bowl of an electric mixer fitted with the paddle attachment, cream the butter and sugar until light and fluffy. Add the eggs, one at a time, then add the vanilla.

4. Add one-third of the flour mixture followed by one-third of the buttermilk and repeat twice more, continuing to mix until all ingredients are fully combined.

(continued on next page)

(continued from previous page)

5.   Divide the batter among the round cake pans and the semi-sphere pans, filling three-quarters of the way.

6.   Bake for 20 to 25 minutes. It may take a bit longer for the semi-sphere cake pans, keep checking every 5 minutes. Let the cakes cool completely.

7.   Meanwhile make the frosting. Chop the chocolate into small pieces, add to a microwave-safe bowl, and microwave at 30-second intervals until fully melted. Set aside.

8.   In the bowl of an electric mixer fitted with the paddle attachment, add the butter and mix on medium-high speed until light and fluffy. Add the egg yolks and vanilla and continue mixing.

9.   Turn the speed to low and add the powdered sugar until fully incorporated. Then add the melted chocolate.

10. In a small bowl, dissolve the coffee granules in the hot water and add to the mixture.

11. Transfer about ¾ cup of the frosting to a small bowl and stir in the red food coloring. Let it sit for a while for the color to mature then add some pink food coloring to create a brighter red. This will be for the inside of the mouth.

12. To assemble the cakes, level the first three layers of the 6-inch (15-cm) round cakes with a serrated knife and stack with frosting in between. Trim to give the stack a teddy body shape, then crumb coat it with the chocolate frosting. Keep all the cake scraps as we will be using them later.

13. Use the leftover top of one of the cakes that you've levelled to give the teddy body a pot belly. Stick it on the front with a little frosting.

14. Use the leftover cake scraps to fill in the gaps between the pot belly and the rest of the body. Add some skewers for stability if needed.

15. To make the head, attach the two semi-sphere cakes together with a little frosting. Crumb coat it and attach it to the body using some bubble tea straws for support.

16. Use all the leftover cake crumbs and a little frosting to make a dough and shape into arms and legs. Attach to the body with some frosting.

17. To decorate: Give the whole teddy another crumb coat. Carve out a large mouth and coat it with the red frosting.

18. Make some round ears with the brown fondant and attach to the head with some skewers or toothpicks (I'd advise you to make these in advance, so they have time to harden).

19. Add the remaining frosting to a piping bag fitted with a grass piping tip. Cover the entire head and body with the chocolate frosting using a grass piping tip to make it look like fur.

20. Shape some of the white fondant into sharp teeth and attach to the inside the mouth with frosting. If they're not sticking use toothpicks.

21. Drip some red food coloring onto the teeth if you'd like your cuddly buddy to be a bit more menacing.

NOTES

If hosting a larger crowd or you just want to make your teddy more intimidating, use five 6-inch (15-cm) round cake pans instead of three. When you get to the batter-filling step, fill them as normal.

In lieu of semi-sphere pans you can use two 6-inch (15-cm) round cake pans. Just stack them together and carve into an oval head shape.

Bewitching Beverages

Skull Boba Bubble Tea

YIELD: Serves 2 ⚶ PREP TIME: 10 minutes, plus 20 minutes rest time ⚶ COOK TIME: 15 minutes

TAPIOCA SKULLS

12 tablespoons tapioca flour
2 tablespoons boiling water

BLACK TEA

5 black tea bags
2 tablespoons granulated sugar
6 tablespoons milk of choice

Bubble tea, also known as boba tea, originated in Taiwan in the 1980s. Its defining feature, the bubbles, are little tapioca pearls that we are converting into skulls for our gothic version. There are many different flavors you can use, but I've gone for a British black tea and oat milk to make this recipe suitable for vegans (although you may use any milk you like).

1. To make the tapioca skulls: In a small bowl, mix the tapioca flour and boiling water with a fork until it forms a dough you can pick up with your hands.

2. Transfer to a clean surface and knead the dough until it becomes smooth.

3. Fill a mini skull (22 mm each) silicone mold with the dough and let it rest for 20 minutes, then unmold.

4. In a medium saucepan, bring about 2 cups (500 ml) of water to a boil. Add the tapioca skulls and cook for 5 minutes or so; you are looking for a soft and chewy consistency.

5. Remove the pan from the heat and let the skulls rest for a few minutes.

6. Transfer the skulls to a bowl of cool water to avoid them sticking together.

7. To make the tea: In a saucepan, add 3 cups (700 ml) of water and bring to a boil. Remove from the heat and add the tea bags and sugar. Stir until the sugar has dissolved, and let the tea steep for 10 minutes, or until the water has come to room temperature.

8. Divide the skulls between two tall glasses, about 1/2 cup (100 g) in each. Top with crushed ice. Pour 1 1/2 cups (355 ml) of the tea into each glass then follow with around 2 to 3 tablespoons of milk. Add more per your preference.

Spiced Hot Chocolate with Chocolate Broomstick Stirrers

YIELD: Serves 4 ⚬ PREP TIME: 2 minutes ⚬ COOK TIME: 20 minutes

HOT CHOCOLATE

½ cup (110 g) packed brown sugar

2 sticks of cinnamon

2 cloves

1 star anise

½ vanilla bean, seeds scraped
   and pod reserved

½ cup (48 g) raw cacao powder

4 cups (960 ml) milk, any kind

Marshmallow fluff, to garnish

BROOMSTICK STIRRERS

4 pretzel sticks

1 cup (175 g) semi-sweet chocolate chips

¼ cup (40 g) white chocolate chips

Last year, I finally fulfilled a little dream—to experience Dia de Los Muertos (Day of the Dead) in Mexico. It was totally worth crossing the Atlantic. The blend of Mayan and Catholic traditions resulted in these vibrant, warming, and original festivities. One of my favorite things about the trip was the hot chocolate served at breakfast. Some may think Mexican hot chocolate has some sort of chilli in it, but it doesn't. I spoke to the chefs at my resort who gave me an idea of what actually gives the hot chocolate its kick. It turns out it is spiced, but not spicy. Additionally, it can be made with any type of milk which is great news for vegans and lactose-intolerant vampires. Add a homemade broomstick stirrer to give this drink extra witchy vibes.

1. To make the hot chocolate: In a large pot, combine 2 cups (475 ml) of water with the brown sugar, cinnamon, cloves, star anise, vanilla bean seeds, half the vanilla pod and the cacao and bring to a boil over medium heat.

2. Reduce the heat, cover, and simmer for about 5 minutes. Remove the lid and let the liquid reduce for 15 to 20 minutes, or until the mixture turns syrup-like. Strain the liquid and discard the spices.

3. Heat up the milk in a medium pan over low-medium heat, do not let it boil. Add the cacao powder. Pour into 4 individual glasses, top with marshmallow fluff, and blowtorch to toast slightly.

(continued on next page)

(continued from previous page)

4. To make the broomstick stirrers: Place 4 pretzel sticks 3 inches apart on a silicone mat.

5. In a heat-proof bowl, add the semi-sweet chocolate chips and microwave at 30-second intervals, stirring in between. Pour into a pastry bag and pipe strings of chocolate on top of the end of the pretzel sticks, covering them. Let them set completely, then peel the entire broomstick off the mat, turn it around and pipe chocolate strands again. This will give the broom a 3D shape.

6. In a heat-proof bowl, add the white chocolate chips and microwave at 30-second intervals, stirring in between. Add a little bit of the semi-sweet chocolate remnants just to color it a lighter brown. Pour into a pastry bag and pipe as the string that ties the bristles together.

7. Add a broomstick atop the torched marshmallow fluff and serve.

TIP | You can forgo the marshmallow and simply sprinkle with a little ground cinnamon before serving with the broomstick.

Nightshade Elixir

YIELD: ½ cup (120 ml) ☽ PREP TIME: 5 minutes, plus 30 minutes infusing time

Bunch of thyme sprigs
¼ cup (60 ml) hot water, not boiling
2 tablespoons apple cider vinegar
2 tablespoons manuka honey
Pinch cayenne pepper

My ideal gothic bakeshop doubles as an apothecary, hence this magical beverage section. This Nightshade Elixir is essentially a homemade cough syrup that not only soothes the lungs and throat for a restful sleep but also tastes pretty good—a quality hard to find in most medicinal options. So good, in fact, I once added oil to it and used it as a salad dressing!

1. Add the thyme sprigs to a standard jam-style jar and cover with the hot water. Add the vinegar, honey, and cayenne, put the lid on tightly, and shake well. Let it infuse for half an hour.

2. Take a tablespoon when needed.

TIP For even more of a health boost, use fire cider instead of apple cider vinegar. Fire cider contains herbs, citrus, roots, and spices to help strengthen the immune system.

Summerween
Lavender and Coconut Mocktail

YIELD: Serves 4 ❦ PREP TIME: 10 minutes, plus 2 hours infusing time

LAVENDER SIMPLE SYRUP

1 cup (250 ml) water
2 cups (400 g) granulated sugar
2 tablespoons dried lavender flower buds

MOCKTAIL

3 cups (720 ml) ice cold water
4 cups (960 ml) coconut water
Juice of 4 to 5 lemons
Purple food coloring

This perfect drink for a witchy Summerween party or BBQ is a variation of my lavender lemonade. Lavender belongs to the same family as rosemary and can be used in the same way—for meat rubs, infusions, or in baking. Lavender is the first herb I ever planted, and I harvest, dry it, and use it all year-round.

1. To make the syrup: In a saucepan, combine the water and sugar and cook over medium heat, stirring until the sugar is fully dissolved. Bring to a boil and remove from the heat. Add the lavender buds.

2. Allow the mixture to infuse for a couple of hours, then strain the syrup through a cheesecloth, squeezing out all the juices.

3. To make the mocktail: In a large jar, combine the lavender syrup, cold water, coconut water, and lemon juice. You can make and add more syrup or lemon juice per your preference.

4. Add a couple drops of the purple food coloring to give a more vibrant hue.

5. Add to a tall glass with ice, decorate with lavender sprigs and/or other edible flowers, spooky stirrers, and serve.

Broken Heart Tea Bomb

YIELD: 2 broken hearts   ❦   PREP TIME: 15 minutes, plus 35 minutes cooling time

⅓ cup (60 g) clear isomalt crystals
Red gel food coloring
2 tea bags of choice
Dried rosebud flowers
Decorative sprinkles
Edible glitter

Have you ever heard of a tea bomb? I suppose they are the tea response to a chocolate bomb. Tea bags or loose tea leaves are encased in a sugar/hard candy shell that dissolves in a cup of boiling water to reveal its contents. Pretty fun, right? The basic tea bomb is made with semi-sphere molds like the ones I use for my Vintage Witch Cakes (page 131), but to lean more into the gothic look we'll be using anatomical hearts. You'll need two molds per heart (each heart approximately 35 mm by 25 mm) in order to make it 3D.

1. In a heat-proof bowl, add the isomalt and microwave at 30-second intervals to melt.

2. Quickly and carefully add a few drops of the red food coloring and mix in with a spoon.

3. Pour enough liquid into your molds to fully cover in a thin layer, spreading it with the back of the spoon. Let it cool completely before unmolding, around 20 minutes.

4. Unmold what will be the bottom halves of the heart and fill each with a tea bag, leaving the strings outside. Also add the dried flowers, sprinkles, and glitter.

5. Place a small skillet over low heat, unmold the top halves of the heart, and place in the skillet open side down. Smooth the edges of the top halves of the heart in the heated skillet and quickly join them with the bottom heart halves. They will not match perfectly, but this will add extra quirk to the look. Allow to cool completely before using, around 15 minutes.

6. Place your heart bombs in glasses or teacups, pour boiling water on top, and let the magic reveal itself!

TIPS

To aid in pouring the isomalt when hot, microwave in a silicone cupcake mold that can be bent.

If you make your own mold for this project (see page 15), make sure to make two opposite sides of the heart so it will match up seamlessly.

Lavender Maple Moon Milk

YIELD: Serves 6 | PREP TIME: 5 minutes | COOK TIME: 8 minutes

2 cups (480 ml) skim milk
2 cups (460 ml) light cream
1 tablespoon lavender buds
1/2 cup (120 ml) maple syrup
1 teaspoon vanilla extract
Pinch freshly ground nutmeg,
    plus more for garnish

Moon milk is so called as it's designed to be taken before bed for a relaxing sleep. Traditionally this drink is made with herbs and spices, but here I've used lavender, long known for its relaxing properties. The added maple flavor is an absolute delight! For a final magical touch, pair with the Lavender Moon Shortbread (page 37).

1. In a saucepan, combine the milk, cream, lavender, syrup, vanilla, and a pincah of nutmeg over low-medium heat.

2. Stir and warm the mixture to just before boiling point. Let it steep for a few minutes, then strain through a mesh sieve lined with cheesecloth into a clean pitcher..

3. Pour into 6 mugs and sprinkle each with freshly grated nutmeg. Enjoy with a moon shortbread cookie.

Herbal Energy Potion

YIELD: Serves 1 ☿ PREP TIME: 5 minutes

1-inch (2.5-cm) piece ginger root
¼ teaspoon ground cardamom
¼ teaspoon ground turmeric
2 teaspoons honey
Hot water, just before boiling point

An herbal alternative to coffee or tea, this is the perfect potion for morning ghouls. Ginger and cardamom have long been proven to improve circulation and boost your metabolism, while turmeric raises energy levels naturally. As a night vampire, I sure need this jumpstart to get me through the morning.

1. In your favorite morning mug, add a couple of thin slices of ginger then peel and juice the rest into the cup.

2. Add the cardamom, turmeric, and honey. Top with hot water and enjoy.

Pumpkin Cream Cold Brew

YIELD: Serves 4   ♦   PREP TIME: 10 minutes, plus 18 to 24 hours chill time

COLD BREW COFFEE

3 ounces (85 g) coffee beans

3 cups (720 ml) cold water

PUMPKIN CREAM

1 cup (240 ml) heavy whipping cream

1/2 cup (120 ml) sweetened condensed milk

2 teaspoons vanilla extract

3 tablespoons pumpkin purée

2 teaspoons pumpkin-pie spice

Brewing coffee cold rather than hot results in a smooth, rich, and less acidic taste. Here we combine our brew with a homemade pumpkin cold foam cream for a perfect autumnal and moody drink.

1. To make the cold brew: Grind the coffee beans to a coarse consistency. In a medium jar or jug, combine the ground coffee and cold water. Stir well to mix, cover, and refrigerate for 18 to 24 hours.

2. Line a mesh sieve with cheesecloth or a coffee filter. Remove coffee from refrigerator and strain into a clean jar. Put the liquid back in the fridge until ready to use.

3. To make the pumpkin cream: Whisk together the cream, milk, and vanilla in a large bowl until fully incorporated. Add the pumpkin purée and pumpkin spice and continue whisking until thick and smooth. Refrigerate until ready to use.

5. Fill 4 glasses halfway with ice, add 1 cup (237 ml) of the cold brew coffee and 1/4 cup (60 ml) of water. In a blender or with a milk frother, whisk 1/4 to 1/2 cup (60 to 118 ml) of the pumpkin cream per glass until fluffy and add on top.

Index

·→· Acknowledgments ·←·

I would like to express my deepest gratitude to everyone who supported me throughout the journey of writing this book and to those who made it happen. Special thanks to my editor, Cara, whose insights, patience, and guidance helped shape these pages into something I'm proud to share. To Rage, for believing there is a big enough market for spooky culinary souls. And to the readers—thank you for picking up this book and letting these elaborate little treats become a small part of your world.

About the Author

Author, baker, and television personality Helena Garcia was born in Spain. Due to her father's job, Helena lived in several cities across Spain, including Madrid, Barcelona, Valladolid, and the Canary Islands, finishing high school in Las Vegas, Nevada. After graduation, she moved back home to Spain to study psychology at the University of Salamanca. Through the EU's study-abroad program, Erasmus, she finished her degree at Leeds University in West Yorkshire, England. After working in several industries, she went back to school to study interior design with the goal of establishing a career in a creative setting. This path led to an opportunity for Helena to take over a beautiful Victorian apothecary, where she developed her own brand of fashion accessories and oddities.

Helena was one of the 2019 *Great British Bake Off* (also known as *The Great British Baking Show)* contestants, winning the hearts of the nation with her eccentric style, spooky approach, and fun-loving personality. She has also appeared in several television shows, including the hit series *What We Do in the Shadows*, and she continues to write for national and international publications.

Obsessed with anything witchy, Helena's self-published book, *Introduction to Witchery: A Magical Guide for Witches that Craft*, is a go-to guide for crafty witches that covers a bit of history of witchcraft in Britain, a guide to magical plants, and plenty of craft projects and recipes to help you live like every day is Halloween. Her second book, *The Wicked Baker*, was released in 2020, followed by *The Witch-Crafting Handbook* in 2021 and *The Book of Gingerbread* in 2023. Her first picture book, *My Mummy is a Witch*, was also published in 2023.

Helena lives in Yorkshire with husband Will, daughter Flora, and rescue wolf-dog Kato.

First published in 2025 by Castle Books, an imprint of The Quarto Group,
142 West 36th Street, 4th Floor, New York, NY 10018, USA
(212) 779-4972 www.Quarto.com

EEA Representation, WTS Tax d.o.o.,
Žanova ulica 3, 4000 Kranj, Slovenia.
www.wts-tax.si

Castle titles are also available at discount for retail, wholesale, promotional, and bulk purchase.
For details, contact the Special Sales Manager by email at specialsales@quarto.com or by mail at The Quarto Group, Attn: Special Sales Manager, 100 Cummings Center Suite 265D, Beverly, MA 01915 USA.

10 9 8 7 6 5 4 3 2 1

ISBN: 978-1-57715-543-0

Digital edition published in 2025
eISBN: 978-0-7603-9711-4

Library of Congress Control Number: 2025936527

Group Publisher: Rage Kindelsperger
Creative Director: Laura Drew
Art Director: Marisa Kwek
Managing Editor: Cara Donaldson
Interior Design: Amelia LeBarron
Author Photo: Felicity Barsky
Food Photography: Lorena Masso
Food Stylists: Victoria Woollard & Lorena Masso
Food Stylist Assistant: Nan Bullock
Prop Stylist: Alessandra Mortola

Printed in Illinois, USA VP062025